MW00966541

RAINBOW
REVOLUTION

UNBLOCK RESISTANCE, CREATE CHANGE AND BE HAPPY WITH YOURSELF

By

BERNARD CHARLES

Copyright © 2017

thecolormage.com

DISCLAIMER: All brand names and product names used in this book are trademarked, registered trademarks, or trade names of their respective holders. The Color Mage and Bernard Charles is not associated with any product or vendor in this book. The information contained in this book is intended for educational and entertainment purposes only. It is not intended to substitute for medical care or to prescribe treatment for any health condition. The Color Mage and Bernard Charles assume no responsibility to or liability for any person or group for any loss, damage, or injury resulting from the use or misuse of any information herein.

No part of this publication may be reproduced, distributed, or transmitted in any form or by any means, including photocopying, recording or other electronic or mechanical methods, without the prior written permission of the publisher, except in the case of brief quotations embodied in reviews and certain other non-commercial uses permitted by copyright law.

Cover and Interior typeface: Colors of Autumn by TattooWoo, Oswald by Vernon Adams, and Julius Sans One by Luciano Vergara

Photography and Design: Bernard Charles

Proofreading: Angela Ekvall

Printed by CreateSpace

All inquiries: please contact *hello@thecolormage.com*

Pumpkin Spell for Love and Abundance

DOWNLOAD THIS POWERFUL VIDEO TRAINING FOR FREE!

READ THIS FIRST

Just to say thank you for buying my book,

I would like to give you a little more magic 100% FREE!

TO DOWNLOAD GO TO:

thecolormage.com/pumpkin

THE SOUL BECOMES DYED WITH THE COLOR OF ITS THOUGHTS

MARCUS AURELIUS

FOR

New Orleans, 1973

Atlanta, 1997

Virginia, 2000

Armenia, 2012

Moscow, 2014

Jerusalem, 2015

Orlando, 2016

And Harvey Bernard Milk

MAY HOPE NEVER BE SILENT

I LIKE LIGHT
COLOR
LUMINOSITY

OSCAR DE LA RENTA

COLORFUL CONTENTS
I solemnly swear, I'm up to only good...

MY COLOR JOURNEY

YOUR COLOR JOURNEY

THE WHOLE WORLD
AS WE EXPERIENCE
IT VISUALLY COMES
TO US THROUGH THE
MYSTIC REALM OF
COLOR

HANS HOFMANN

BUILD A STRONGER YOU WITH THE POWER OF LOVE, LIGHT AND COLOR

Are you ready?

The world is saturated with people too afraid to be themselves. Fearful to be seen, unapologetically unhappy and resistant to love. I see most people resentful toward themselves for hiding behind other people's decisions and choices about their lifestyle and identity. I'm tired of poverty. I'm tired of religious babble. I'm tired of walking down the street feeling uninspired because droves of sleepwalkers choose mindless conformity over awakened consciousness. These are dark times that require heroes. Individuals who aren't afraid to come together. Emerge as one. Rebuild the world using the power of color. This is the start of a new you and a new way to live. It's a revolution.

In seven weeks, I challenged myself to connect with color in a new way. Create and alter sacred space in order to get my life back on track after a break up. Give my bedroom and brain an energy cleanse at the same time. This book contains my deepest core values and colorful insights that I'm sharing with you so that you can rebuild a relationship with yourself, infuse power with the ordinary, and retrieve the strength to live outside the lines of fear. By exploring the influence of color since 2007, I notice shifts in how I show up in the world and my everyday choices are more intuitive and less fear-based.

For example, I'm choosing not to wear certain clothes that hide my body out of some deep hidden seed of self-hatred. I'm no longer biting my nails because I don't see a certain amount of my money in the bank account. I stopped hanging out with people who bring me down and steal my energy. Color gives me boundaries and prompts me to live life on my own terms.

In this spiritual journey challenge for myself, I gathered specific objects based on my color needs and this practice shifted my perspective on how balance (some people call it chi) plays out in my private and professional life. I started noticing interesting things happen beyond my meditation space like getting compliments from strangers on the streets, falling in love with the real me and being featured as a color expert in *Soul & Spirit Magazine*.

This isn't a fluffy aura book. Nor is it a high-brow encyclopedia on the science of color. I'm not going to ramble on about color theory. I don't pretend to be real; I am real. This book is a battle cry for you to activate your real power using color and everyday objects in whatever space you find yourself in to ignite a force from within and around your own body, mind and soul. You don't need to see auras to make this challenge work for you. And you don't need to know all the psychological motives behind color to feel what you feel. Color is personal and unique to you. It's through my own journey, I guide you to seeing color in a new way and use your greatest power of all, intuition by feeling how color influences your body, mind and soul as you use it to create your reality. This book is intentionally set up so that you take a bold approach to color that fights fear and finds peace.

All intentions manifest in some shape and form. Take your time and sit in the company of your own space. Your presence is life-changing. You'll see through my own colorful journey that I've been jobless, heartbroken and homeless. I've lived out of suitcases and garbage bags for most of my life. It's now in my late 20s that I'm finally building my own roots and finding that sense of home I've struggled to feel.

Spoiler alert:
Home is where you feel like a commodity not an oddity. And you're allowed to have more than one.

Because everything happens for a reason, I feel that overcoming all of my ridiculous adversities have been one huge blessing to expand my awareness of color and deepen the magic inside this revolution. Inspiring a soul tribe of people who dare to be different to continue coloring this world with their own strength and voice.

It's within this community that gives people a home for their soul and the permission to share their natural magic freely (as long as it doesn't harm or persecute others). I was never one to spew pompous academic views when it comes to magic or religion like you see on *Tumblr* or in your own church. People who do look down at others in such a way are vile creatures indeed. Color is non-denominational, so nothing you'll be doing in this revolution is sin or evil. You'll triumphantly deepen your connection to the extraordinary source inside of you, sacred space, and the tools you decide to use along your way.

This is a guide to building and cleansing a happy place through color. Providing you with key elements to construct, tend and feel the power of using your creative energy. No, you don't have to be an artist or certified in any metaphysical education to be a part of this movement. Accessing and reflecting on this energy in a new way may offer deep emotional breakthroughs and prepare you for those divine moments that we in the industry call synchronicity or a-ha moments. It's by building your space with power and color that influences your outcomes and options.

Perhaps you already create altars for each lunar cycle or keep a space above the fireplace to commemorate the ashes of your undying love, this book is still for you because it's a new journey of self-discovery. You are meant to be reading this right now. We are meant to walk this path together so you can retrieve that sacred treasure and personal happiness that only safe space offers.

It's a very dark time to be going at life solo. Pretending that a spiritual journey is meant to be lonely or believing that you're cursed to never find love again because up until this point you've been rejected and heartbroken is complete bullshit. Ego and fear will do anything to keep you blind from the truth. You're invited as soon as you open this book to come and sit among a community of friends you never knew you had that want to respect your place in this world. Honor your humanity. And pour honeysuckle sweetness over your wounds. We all drank from the same magic pool to come here and now it's time we remember to find love, build our light and color the world with all our might.

I ask you again, are you ready?

Beautiful! Let me share with you who I am and what prompted this personal and sacred revolution. So you have a better understanding about taking this journey yourself. I know real action scares people, but I trust you're the type of person that loves getting results out of the blue and isn't afraid to take responsibility to change your life for good.

BEHIND THE REVOLUTION

I'm ordinary. I was never popular in school. I took summer school twice. I told my English teacher and any other condescending authority in the world to fuck off. I'm a bat out of hell soul. I'm the kid who wore his sister's jeans to school and was suspended for speaking the truth. I fumble over my words when I'm passionate. I'm the one who rouses your inner rebel to quit your day job and pursue a better-looking world. I'm the shepherd who cares for black sheep because the white ones fear the sparkle of my coat with many colors. I'm living proof of what I preach. I was born into a Catholic family but altar hopped among Christian denominations with my grandmother after my parents divorced in 2000. I went to college because everyone told me to. I'm the owner of 800+ rejection letters from employers who refused to give me a chance. It looks like the obligation to pay your dues and debt isn't enough for this world. And still people on this planet choose to see me through their dark shady fear-glasses since I don't dim my own light anymore. I don't cower in their shade. I choose to shine outside of shame.

I'm multi-passionate and some say it's my Achilles' heel because I don't blindly accept what we are handed. I question and judge using color as my guide. I paved the way for people like you to see beyond the looking glass. Making colorful connections and recognizing patterns in the world that elevates our evolution.

Does the pursuit of self-development and enlightenment even matter? Yes, but not for appearing ultra-spiritual or deceiving millions through glamorized spirituality. Assholes still can do yoga. Bandwagon bitches can still sell herbs and crystals. This revolution is about realizing your creative power to build a meaningful life even if it means ruffling a few feathers. Hell-bent on seeing the world beyond gray, I've fought to set the world on fire with my light and resurrected deep power so that we together become the force that darkness fears the most. Color is my mantra and and authenticity is my motivation. It bites sometimes, but that's life.

Yup, so because the world told me I wasn't good enough and that I didn't offer any reinforcement of it's already messed up institution, I decided to be a rebel and give people their life back through reading color and creating a legendary color card deck called *The Color Mage Oracle.* It's this rainbow altar journey that unblocked most of the energy I needed to experience my identity to my higher self and create something that matters so that the world would be able to understand the magic and meaning behind their own intuition using color as their spellbook.

Up until this challenge, I lived quietly and dared not to push the gas pedal on my dreams, emotions or my thoughts to change the world. I didn't really have a particular talent for focusing on socially accepted ambitions like everyone else . I sold myself short by believing in other people's opinions of me. Forcing me to accept how my heart was wrong for loving the same-sex, admitting I'm really just a free-loader because

I didn't have a real job as a start-up spiritual practitioner, or that I needed to stop wasting my time with self-development. It seemed like I was born into a world resistant to my light. Offended by my millennial purity and genuine acceptance that love trumps fear. Yet, I learned through coloring my life to keep the lights on even in dark times. Adapt to the foul snooty citizens of this world and serve love despite the thickness or size of one's ego.

Because I'm extraordinarily different (I know you don't have to tell me twice), I experienced a nasty double breakup in 2013. One that resulted in my search for self-compassion (a romantic prologue with subtle miracles that you'll read about in my chapter on the power of green and pink) and the second (non-romantic just your typical family baggage about a gossip-thirsty woman who's too far up her own ass to care authentically) being of no particular value besides that I spot stupid quicker now. Both situations guided me to become my own boss and live unapologetic for my deep devotion to my individual soul path.

In two months after deciding to be a meditation coach and read color professionally, I met a man because I worked my own Fairy Godmother skills and created a pumpkin spell for love and abundance. It's between that DIY pumpkin ritual and the power of red that would change the course of my spiritual journey. I spent the majority of 2014 with a man whose expectations I allowed to distract me from my power and value. He insisted on judging me because I didn't have a normal job (meditation coaching and color readings are way too different for some people), my own car, or an apartment to practice real adulting. So I decided to swallow my pride that summer for this man and get a normal job as a work-at-home customer service representative so that I could get the car, the place and final approval on my self-worth.

One night he asked me to come over and when I got there I found a strange guy inside his bed. And my excitement to see him rapidly deflated. Seeing the scenes playback inside my mind, I could feel the pulse of the walls. I forced myself into the bathroom, turned the sink on full blast and started talking to my reflection.

What the fuck was happening? Is this seriously happening right now? The guy fucking looks like me. That fucking no-name guy is on my side of the bed and he looks like me.

Jealousy and rage boiled inside. I didn't want to believe this was happening to me. I let my emotions churn like a storm on the sea as I washed my hands vigorously to waste time. I wanted to deny everything I was feeling. I wanted to rewind time and refuse the offer to visit. But there I was hunched over the sink staring at the rainbow highlighted soap suds dancing down the drain.

Over the years, I learned to compact my emotions and keep them hidden until I found a safe space to sort through my life's happenings. Mastering the art of processing which is just a fanciful way of saying, let me meditate and cool the fuck down.

I hung onto every second I could in the bathroom taking deeper breaths as I stared at my reflection. I splashed my face with some water to re-center and held back any sign of tears. I didn't yell or make a scene like you would see on T.V.

It wasn't very dramatic at all. Remember I'm ordinary. All of this was very unexpected and I was trying to process every last emotion, word and give myself a thorough play-by-play.

What did I miss? Were there red flags or giant bill-board moments telling me what was ahead but, I was too naive and distracted by coloring his picture of me? Do I even have an intuition considering that I couldn't prevent this from happening by catching it quicker?

Questions spiraled to unanswered places.

There wasn't any indication he had company when he texted me because he didn't mention it. There weren't any signs he was seeing other people because our conversations were never equal. He looked at me like I wasn't qualified to have an opinion as his *partner*. I lacked sufficient life experience and funds to be anything meaningful. I felt the high he got from traveling and flexing those "availability" muscles that I see most gay men display on dating apps and at chic events. I felt the debris of his past orbiting his body, mind and soul. So I stayed for as long as I could trying to heal a man I gen-uinely loved and cared for by being present. Not in an overly rambunctious way. I quietly held room for this Cancer man to stop whining about his life and just let love in. That's hard for a lot of people I find. Because our souls did recognize each other instantly which you'll find out about soon, I was willing to let some things go. But as we see I didn't have what he wanted, only time, but not even that seems to be enough in this world.

I felt violated and used that night. Strung along emotionally, I realized that trying to build your life based on someone else's opinion steals your identity and self-worth. You're enslaved by their ideals and desires to measure how well you're performing as a human in their life saga. And depending on the timing you just won't be able to fulfill those needs and obligations because mostly, what they truly seek could never be found outside of themselves. This doesn't mean you stop loving, it means you start living ruthlessly authentic. Interdependently and interconnected with your own relationship to yourself, others and the world.

It's called respecting one's autonomy.

When I eventually came out of the hot and steamy bathroom, I asked when and where they met. And I got this grand happy story of them meeting at one of the summer gay camp events. Neurons fired inside my brain immediately as I felt my eyebrow raise in disbelief. I planned on going to that very same event. But I didn't go because I had to work that weekend for that unnecessary customer service job that I only took to please someone's opinion of me. *See what's happening here?* Putting people on a pedestal and having them not do the same for you is a major inequality issue. I was pissed at myself for building a life around a man who already had a life and no problem playing all sides of the fence. It hurt and I had no one to tell (until now). I was alone in my own thoughts, heartbroken and within nanoseconds handed this fake relationship over to a source greater than myself.

That night, I stayed over. I didn't leave because my ego wanted to stick it out. And eventually, that wannabe-me-dude left because he wasn't feeling so well. *Bye Felicia.* Perhaps my aura was a tad bit too much to handle that night. I remember sliding into my side of the bed, rolling over to sleep and as soon as the lights went out, I released a small pocket of tears I stubbornly held back all night. The following morning we fooled around. It was the best sex in awhile. It felt right to finish strong and leave in a signature way.

After we finished, he smiled at me so I asked about his plans for the day hoping to segue into what had happened last night and my feelings. But I saw his body tense up and he started explaining he had to meet his son for church. So I watched him get ready and made it a point to compliment his clothing choice for the day. I remember him telling me that I never complimented him enough so to right some wrongs, I did that morning. It was colorful and fit for him. He leaned over his bed before leaving and we hugged. My bare skin glowing against the fabric of his rigid clothes reminded me of how open and vulnerable my idealism is against the textured world. Time stood still that morning. He softly told me *thank you*. I didn't try to over analyze or latch onto his words too much. I looked into his ice blue eyes and replied, *I'll miss you*. He sauntered off to seize the day while I made my way to the shower.

A part of me knew this would be the last time I would see him. So, I took care of leaving his space energetically sound by cleaning his dishes in the sink and dusting off his crystal arrangement he keeps near the door. After I felt like the space was renewed by my natural touch, I locked the door behind me. It was on my way out when I saw a ruby-throated hummingbird hovering over one of his magenta colored hibiscus flowers.

This was a clear sign offering me a color-coded message.

I'm to enjoy the nectar of my own legacy that comes from what gives me joy.

I learned even in these struggles and life transitions, the Divine is always there watching our life. Living it with us. We have to be open to seeing the signs when life feels too vast and chaotic to understand. This was a blessing in a disguise.

People choose many coping strategies and mechanisms to help them bounce back from the color of life bruising their assumptions or expectations. I'm sure you have your own memory and story about a time you built your life around something or someone only for it to fall short of what you had hoped. We build up an image of our parents, then their true colors slip through our filters and it shocks us. On the other hand, parents create ideas about their children before they're born, so when their projections and expectations aren't met, they become unnerved and lodged in lifelong cycles of criticism and skepticism as a way to punish the child subconsciously.

We even place lovers and idols on very high platforms in our minds. When they slip on the piety that we superimpose onto their aura, we throw a tantrum. The media loves to profit on this kind of gossip the most. We become addicted to our own miserable darkness that we created ourselves because it feels so good and right to our ego. And who wants to feel wrong? No one.

But there are those that walk among us everyday that think a little more colorful. A group of people all over the world that aren't hosting pity parties. They are actively creating their own way: Choosing love over fear. Improvising real miracles.

Embracing the opportunity to adapt and innovate one's life. Thinking outside of the box. Creating a new normal for themselves and the people they love regardless of material status. Unlocking resistance. Being the change. And this is the real spiritual transformation. We are the revolutionaries that the world needs most. We are the trailblazers and inventors. The leaders and dreamers. We are a conscious collective who finds acceptance and meaning in all color. Not just the ones that make our ego look beautiful. But humanity brave.

Take this challenge to actively color your life in a new way. Use it to invoke power, confidence, love and freedom to express yourself. In the coming chapters, you'll relive seven of my life-changing milestones with color that swiftly restored my faith in the world, turned on my abundance mindset, healed broken relationships, and gave me the energy needed to make miracles happen by paying attention to the power of color in my life.

While building your perfect altars keep the five major elements (theme, location, decoration, upkeep and alteration) in mind and let the weekly writing prompts inspire deep spiritual and emotional breakthroughs. And I promise you'll discover a new way to color in this world that's not based on incorporated trends or defaulting to a favorite color because that's how society wants you to feel about your identity.

Speaking of brainwashing identities, I'm judging everyone who does a gender reveal using pink for girls and blue for boys when it fact, you're not revealing the gender. You're revealing the baby's sex. Gender isn't binary nor can it be diluted into two colors. Rant over. No one has time for that – grab a friend, we have revolution to build.

School is very conformist and one of the very first conforming that goes on in preschool and kindergarten is gender

Dan Savage

BASIC TRAINING AND TERMINOLOGY

All ruby slipper wearing revolutionaries deserve basic training. Here I'll define keywords and give you a brief (bare naked no fluff) breakdown on the terms and tools I use daily to stay fierce. It's very gaily forward. There aren't fancy methods or previous experience required for the challenge, but knowing what I'm about to share with you will help you connect the dots with a juicy thick marker instead of a dried out one from the 90s. If you find yourself lost at any point remember to ask your questions in the Rainbow Revolution book club: http://bit.ly/rainbowrevolution

CHAKRAS

You'll see throughout this book I mention chakras. Now, my spin on the word is pretty basic. And I don't intend on diluting the history or meaning behind these vortexes of natural light that support your body's aura, but I do want you to be aware of the chakra system to better understand how certain colors, intuitive messages and life moments tend to reveal a certain personality or quality to your journey through color. It's like a cheat sheet for the archetypal energy you'll be following to find enlightenment through this altar building process. So for the purpose of this book and your own spiritual revolution, know that chakras are energy points and depending on the color you're working with will give you clues about what chakra you're energizing or ignoring in your personal and professional life.

I'm keeping these so easy you won't forget! There are seven main chakras. And seven colors. Plus two, gotta have pink, oh and shimmer! This is a very simple structure to avoid over-complicating your color journey. And it's a fun way to spot chakra energy when you're out in the monotonous world. Color is the secret password and knowing the chakras is like knowing which house you're entering in *Hogwarts*. Minus the talking paintings.

RED for the root chakra
ORANGE for the navel chakra
YELLOW for the solar plexus chakra
GREEN AND PINK for the heart chakra
BLUE for the throat chakra
PURPLE for the third eye chakra
WHITE for the crown chakra

Here's a tip: If you want to amplify your crown chakra vibration, add metallic energy like silver or a really sweet holographic coloring. It carries a multidimensional effect to connect with the all spiritual realms. Um, is that a unicorn behind you?

SACRED SPACE

Everyone occupies space. It's in how we maintain one's space that makes it sacred or not. Clutter, dust and heaps of habitual hoarding is not sacred. It's messy and disruptive to your energy. Sacred Space is personal for each and every individual. You can discover it in nature, at home, in a secret corridor at work or inside the meditation realms of prayer and dreams. You are the housekeeper and the gatekeeper to this place and it's this place that must feel sacred. Safe.

Our own book club acts like the Room of Requirement (get ready for some major *Harry Potter* action all up in this book because the army is real). Sacred space is a magical place to gather and practice your own charms and spiritual skills. Meditate and pray. Connect with witches and wizards all over the world in body, mind and soul.

CRYSTALS

There are thousands of crystals and whole encyclopedias already dedicated to the subject. If you wanna learn more, check out the resources section where I list books and people that have transformed my relationship to crystals and my spiritual practice. Just to squeeze this in, I started dabbling in my spiritual journey with two crystals (quartz and amethyst) that I bought at an art museum . If you can't find crystals check museum gift shops! I used these to awaken my mind and stop feeling the pressure to conform in high school. And connect with the almighty source during final exams week. I let my crystals soak up those study vibes and when the test came around I placed the crystals on my desk to support my clarity and memory. I felt my intuition expand. I highly recommend you get these basic crystals before finishing this book. You'll turn up your vibe and remember how powerful you are in this Universe. Do work with them regularly to build that energetic rapport. Don't leave them somewhere expecting to be cool just because you have crystals.

Respect the craft.

MAGIC

Color is a powerful sinless kind of magic. The pursuit to color my life path was a brave leap into very unknown territory. I didn't hear of anyone else doing this sort of thing. Coaching people to live more through the power of color? Nope. But then as I started to read people in a new way it took off. My intuition strengthened and I became known as The Color Mage. It's this rainbow altar experience that unlocked the energy I needed to breakthrough and create the largest most powerful color therapy oracle deck in the world. And it was the right amount of prep work for my energy, when I needed to feel peace with major loss at the end of 2014 because my grandmother died and plans fell through trying to move into my own apartment. This journey is the bedrock to getting out of my own way and living completely on my passions with a purpose to bring more color into the world.

Now, that's real magic!

ESSENTIAL OILS

When I began my journey, I should have gotten involved sooner with essential oils and chemical-free plant based products. This is in hindsight. I never experienced with crystals or cards what these oils do for me. It's a big disappointment that people look at essential oils as some scheme or scam. Scams are what you find with dirt cheap pricing and poor farming conditions forcing you to remain small and fearful in the out-dated capitalism as a blind consumer. I'm blessed to be part of my essential oil company. It's a major part of keeping my promise in raising the vibration of the world one color at a time (or in this case one oil at a time).

You using toxic chemicals isn't only damaging your energy, it's also ignorantly poisoning your family and the world. Being able to streamline my cleaning, vitamins/supplements and personal care products like toothpaste and mouthwash not to mention my essential oils is a huge return on my investment emotionally and spiritually. I'm more than a consumer, I'm a globally conscious citizen leveraging wellness, abundance and purpose.

WANDS AT THE
READY
THE RAINBOW
REVOLUTION
WANTS YOU
BERNARD CHARLES

PART ONE
My Color Journey

THE POWER OF RED

The color red energizes the root or the base chakra. And it's this color that most marketers use to get you as a consumer to feel impulsive. Take action. But it's also the color of romance and love. While building my own altar, I found it easy to pull together my red items. Red isn't that hard to spot, but I do know some may struggle with this color as it's not easily seen especially if you're color blind. Or you're super offended by the color's historical attachment to extremists, blood and fear. This color naturally provokes feelings of fight or flight and many animals and some plants have this color to communicate warnings, threats or danger for survival purposes. Like the saying goes, see red you're dead.

However, I have a different association with this color energy and it begins with meeting that man who spurred on this need to rebuild my life. Yup, the Cancer guy with dirty dishes and dusty crystals. We met at a Gay and Lesbian conference because this Cinderella went rogue and did a pumpkin spell for love and abundance. Two weeks after the ritual I performed, I got news of the conference being held downtown but I only had $15 in my bank account.

The exact amount it would cost me to attend, I took it as a sign. This was a challenge the Divine presented to me as I believe that when we cast a prayer or ritual, the Divine tests our faith so that we have the chance to face our demons and overcome a fear specifically attached to our desired outcome. To go or not to go. To fear lack of money or invest in my own empowerment and real abundance regardless of how much money I have to my name. Cinderella decided to go to the ball that day.

I just finished my meditation certification and wanted to put myself out there more in the community as a reliable and gay-friendly resource. And on the morning of the event, I pulled the color red intuitively for my color of the day. So I decided to wear my red pants and go to the event. When I got there I felt noticed. No one else was rocking red pants. Most people looked dark and miserly wearing shades of blue and black. I suppose I was expecting a little more from the LGBT community. I mean after all pride fests are always colorful. Small town culture can be quite concrete and ashy. Oh how I wish every town was festive and interesting like the events and people from the *Gilmore Girl* village of Stars Hallow. I guess people just don't wake up most days feeling vibrant and beautiful (this is another reason the world needs color).

I walked myself over to the refreshments, grabbed some cranberry juice and sat at table 11. On purpose I like to choose angel numbers like 11, 22, 44, or 33. It makes me feel magical and miraculous. You may have seen the online sphere go nuts over posting photos of 11:11 or 444. It's a numerical practice that new agers use to affirm synchronicity or messages from the angels. It's really fun for me and I don't let myself get too bogged down by trying to make these digital affirmations happen. You know when something is a sign or not. One doesn't force spirit, magic or prayer to bend to one's will. You simply ask in faith, show up to face fear and allow the blessing to manifest. By doing so you become open to experiencing the divine's power live through you and around you.

I made myself comfortable at table 11 which happens to be in the center of the ballroom and waited for the event to begin. I was listening to the opening remarks when I started to feel a presence. I remember thinking to myself. Someone is watching me. This feels hot, wild and delicious and it's piercing my concentration. And there I turn to my left and see this blonde haired man shooting arrows my way. It was intense and I felt turned on by the connection. After the welcome presentations ended, I made my way to my first workshop. A seminar on sexually transmitted infections. I appreciate the intent of education, but that workshop left me feeling like I had one – and I wasn't even sexually active!

After the terrifying talk on surviving and living free from STIs, a mass exodus formed (I wasn't the only one relieved to get out of there) and marched it's way back to the ballroom so we could enjoy lunch in peace. I stopped at the refreshment table again and chugged four cranberry juices this time because I was so flushed from battling fearful thoughts, I took one look at my pants and it occurred to me that maybe wearing red and attending a talk on potentially life-threatening diseases was a little too much to bear. I finished my last cup of juice, walked back to my table and waited to be served by grumpy looking people trapped inside black uniforms.

I had just finished my vegetable medley when I started to feel my every move being monitored and tracked. Noticing this intense inquisitive presence again, I looked up from my plate and sure enough it was that same man checking me out. I scooped bits of my broccoli and pretended to not notice (being coy with my own mind) because I knew that he knows that I know he's locked interest on me. I felt ignited and very seen. Being noticed by someone you're attracted to is quite a fresh feeling. It burns calories just feeling the desire, infatuation and lust. I felt the room melt as I tasted this man's red delicious aura. A warm cinnamon glaze baked inside me. My appetite grew but my plate was empty.

I handed my dish to the nearest server, adjusted myself and waited for my own aura to stop throbbing. An announcement for the next round of workshops came over the microphone and so I escorted myself from the table. I made my way just before the lobby doors, when I hear a man's voice tell me that I dropped my pen. I turn to see that one of the event volunteers was holding my red pen. Flushed for thinking it was someone else, I claimed my note-taking pen and said thank you. As I was smiling in gratitude, I flung a glance over to see that fox was watching the entire exchange. Intently. I threw a smile at him, turned for the door, and let my red pants do the rest.

I took a lot of notes in this second workshop hopping from one side of the paper to the next. It was a talk on being out in the community and creating safe space. I kept quiet like a rabbit grazing on small blades of grass so I could recover from exerting so much energy at lunch. Then as the seminar wrapped up, I saw that sly fox standing in the back as I made my way to the door to leave. I saw him talking to someone else, but our eyes locked on anyway and I smiled. I stopped just outside the door and gave the Universe a serious ultimatum in nanoseconds.

I took a few deep breaths and screamed inside my head.

WHAT AM I DOING? GOD, GODDESS, UNIVERSE WHOEVER IS LISTENING, I'M GOING TO STAND HERE AND IF THIS MAN STOPS AND INTRODUCES HIMSELF THEN I KNOW IT'S FATE.

I looked at my phone after demanding a sign from the Universe and that's when I heard his voice.

He introduced himself, I replied in kind and we made it just outside the door to the last seminar but never walking inside. We stood in the lobby chatting about life, politics and what I did for a living for 90 minutes. This was the first time with authority and conviction I proudly shared what I did as a color reader to a complete stranger. I mentioned the power of color and living authentically. His eyes widened with curiosity. I told him that I think we are meant to be here and asked him if I could read his color on the spot. So I did and his color appeared as red. He laughed. I explained what it meant again thinking he was confused but he still looked at me in disbelief. Then I asked why was he looking at me like that.

He shuffled through a folder and turned over his workshop notes. All I saw was red. I thought I was dead.

Even though I wouldn't foresee his philanderer ways until later, I value this experience to it's core because it pushed me to overcome scarcity, embrace desire and fuel passion in the moment. It's the nature of red that provokes our wild imaginations and pumps life into our choices.

I choose love.

Red hot burning passion over the martyrdom people settle for because they become addicted to their sufferings and painful memories. Red frees a soul by invoking your inner phoenix to rise. Victimhood is boring.

Resisting the temptation to be admired as a damsel in distress for exaggerating the role of prey. Tap into your own predator mindset who survives beyond the pain. Red is a provocative power color that attracts attention and energizes motives and intentions. It's not a color for the weak.

In an effort to cleanse my own mind and life, I needed this color revolution for myself. I spent a lot of time with this man but my identity was rapidly changing as I continued to share the power of color with others. Eventually, I discovered we weren't on the same rose-colored pages anymore. He wanted other men. So I decided to focus on my own journey and allow this challenge to heal the deeper parts of me that I couldn't see.

On my red altar, the deep burgundy color of the rose drew me closer to the real me that must live beyond fear. I could feel the relationship to myself expand with ideas that color passion and deeply accept that I'm a desirable being even if I'm single forever. Interestingly enough my altar was set up in the relationship section of my room according to the bagua map used in traditional feng shui.

By divinity this all came together naturally as I had no intentions on following the bagua when I first started, but after experiencing this I recommend using it now when building your sacred space. You can arrange your entire home using this ancient practice to balance your energy.

I know the pressure one feels to be desirable and sexy. Needing a partner to validate your power. Or hanging onto memories you shared with your exes because you feel guilty it didn't work out and now they're gone. It's self-induced because we strive to belong and feel wanted. Fulfill our fantasies. Assuming if we just have a boyfriend or girlfriend then all our problems will be resolved. Nope.

Romance isn't the magical answer like society would condition us to believe. Mr and Mrs Right comes from your higher power. And your higher power is you. That red hot divinity your body hungers for is real, if you allow yourself to feel the heat of the moment. And if there is someone delicious spooning you or holding your hand, then passionately without judgment love them like a romance novel. This life is meant to be lived not feared. Red is a powerful transfusion color for your soul's path and renews your relationship to raw desire.

I FOUND I COULD SAY THINGS WITH COLOR AND SHAPES THAT I COULDN'T SAY ANY OTHER WAY THINGS I HAD NO WORDS FOR

GEORGIA O'KEEFFE

THE POWER OF ORANGE

The color orange is the life-force of the navel chakra. Many artists and creative types feel pulled to this color energy because it makes them feel happy and alive. It's also the color that saved my life. My spiritual journey with color started in 2007 when I was part of a high school art club that took field trips to museums. It was at an art museum in Philadelphia specializing in found objects where I discovered my brave flamboyant orange scarf that gave me the life-force needed to acknowledge and embrace my sexuality.

I struggled with my sexual identity in school and at home because people didn't accept me and repeatedly bullied me because I was different. It's apparently okay for a penis and a vagina to date, go to prom and be the figurehead of society's perfect couple. Yet, it's socially wrong for same-sex attraction (penis meets penis or vagina meets vagina) to exist? Being LGBT (that's lesbian, gay, bisexual and transgender in case you're living under a rock in the new millennia) isn't wrong and heterosexuals know this deep inside their crotch but they're so wrapped up in fear and illusions pretending this kind of love is immoral when love at it's core is unconditional. Resistance to the LGBT world is cynicism of why we exist in the first place.

When family, school administration and peers forced me to comply with heteronormative conditions by bullying me, I faced a lot of suicidal thoughts. I wanted to give up trying to live in this world that hates me so much that it has to poke at all my colors.

"Yo, FAG, why are you so skinny?"

"You talk like a girl."

"Hey, he-she you're so gay."

All the harassment and hetero-standards put me on the edge. I felt angry toward myself and others! Every day the taunting hardened my heart. I found myself in the guidance counselor's office multiple times a day crying because noth-ing about my life felt happy. I didn't feel like I belonged here and that's when I started picturing what the world would look like without me. How my mom would react. And God knows, I love my mom more than anything. She loves me for me, but between my struggles and the weight of us living in poverty I had to make the decision to get myself out of that sickening mindfucked excuse of a town. It was raping my self-worth. So I asked to apply to a boarding school for children in low-income situations. It's here I started over suicide-free. Now, if you are struggling with suicide, you deserve love - please call the *Trevor Lifeline at 866-488-7386*. Suicide is the second leading cause of death among our young beautiful souls ages 10-24[1].

Heteronormativity is a privilege heterosexuals unknowingly posses. It has similar affects that white privilege presumes upon race but this focuses on straight vs any other sexuality not straight, binary romance and creating a relationship culture skewed to favor heterosexuality in society. Being a proud member of any part of the LGBT spectrum means you're natural. And a necessary part to human evolution.

Dr. James O'Keefe spoke at *TEDxTallaght in Dublin* and gave a moving talk on homosexuality being a natural gift to keeping the human species alive. Prenatal conditions influence the outcome and I can attest to this being true because I was born into a very aggressive and impoverished household. The stress that my mother had to endure while being pregnant with me by our immediate family and also the globalized violence in the 90s, is a no brainer as to why I am the way I am. I'm here to even out the aggression and deepen the soul healing all over the world. My mom needed a fellow Aries to rock the boat back in favor of balance. I'm not an expert in epigenetics or biology.

Biology is one of the classes I failed and had to take in summer school. I don't care about genes. I was more fascinated by the color of biological structures in man and plants than figuring out how likely it is to have a genetic disorder. O'-Keefe's connection to his own son is moving and I recommend if you're still feeling like homosexuality is some contrived religious sin, think again. Being gay is one of Mother

Nature's oh so fabulous secret family recipes for creating more love and less war.

I don't care if you're gay, straight or the flying purple people eater. I believe you were the strongest sperm to get inside that egg and you're meant to be here. The odds were in the trillions but you shifted that creative willpower baby and we get to have your sexy ass face here in the world. Boo ya! Like eclectic art pieces, be open to feeling found because there's nothing better than allowing your true identity to shine like the burning sun. Baby, it's that zesty courage that invigorates more bravery. If this color can give me so much life, just imagine what it can do for you.

Go get yourself an orange scarf and give the world all of that mighty confidence I know you carry inside your DNA.

I only had myself and the power of color during those dark days of bullying to teach me things like authenticity and courage. Some people in my life were there to support me best they could (like my mom and a guidance counselor), but this was my own battle. My soul wanted to feel true and empowered and sometimes you have to accept that your parent or adult isn't going to be there to fight the darkest of demons. You will have to face the fear head on. That's brave. It's not easy whatsoever but it's that courage that floods darkness with radical tangy light.

While I waited for my peers to finish their museum tour, I stood inside the gift shop. I felt a presence there and I knew I had to buy something with my twenty bucks. You'd be surprised how much found objects go for but I didn't have enough money to cover most of the things that tickled my ego. So instead I closed my eyes and asked God to show me what I was suppose to buy. My eyes flung open and I turned around and saw a beautiful rack of scarves. A rainbow flooded my vision and I reached out touching an excited and youthful orange scarf. As soon as I wrapped myself up in it's fabric, I could feel a column of light fill the room. I was having my *Harry Potter* moment. And this scarf would be my wand.

The orange scarf became my sidekick throughout high school and college. It's been the ice breaker in conversations and the sword to all the madness I would endure for the next decade. The biggest breakthrough I've had because of this orange scarf is the confidence and co-creative willpower it gave me when I was homeless because of a family fight. I got evicted out of spite. Morons do that when their narrow-minded ego seeks revenge instead of forgiveness. And I had only one choice and that was to take refuge in my spirituality that day more than I had ever done before. Usually people see being spiritual as a perfect picture of succulents in a post on *Instagram,* doing yoga every Saturday or shitting a lot of rainbows by the pool. Not for me, I have to face this devil in drag and overcome my adversity head first through my spirituality. It's not glamorous. It's real.

Orange not only reminds me of my I-gotta-put-on-a-hard-hat-happiness but also the resourcefulness it takes to land on your feet after the rug has been pulled from under you. Life is unexpected at times, and I surely didn't see this one coming. So because I was homeless I needed to act as quickly and confidently as possible. Luckily, for the past year before this happened, I made true friends in town through my color and essential oils business so that kept me afloat during this traumatic chapter of my life.

This family brawl was very violent to the point of a knife threatening my safety and me not being able to breathe since I had fat arms wrapped around my face. I still don't fully understand why family does this sort of thing but it's happening in homes everywhere. 1.6 million youth every year become homeless. 40% of youth that are homeless identity as LGBT[2]. The youth homelessness rate for LGBT is very high and not many have a support system in place considering one doesn't actually prepare for family conflict or being kicked out. There's some, but not enough effort on resolving this issue.

Because of my own situation, I learned that in my town there was only one men's shelter and the person who managed it first-hand was completely sexist. I called to stay there but he mistaken me for a woman (this happens all the time on the phone - over it) and when I had my friend get on the phone and try to explain the situation more clearly since I was caught up in emotions at this point, he was arrogant and rude. Spouting off how boys don't know how to speak up for themselves and they have women like my friend speaking in their place. Then what really irritated me was that he used to be homeless himself and still was empty of any compassion toward this situation. It was a nightmare because this was the only resource I had as a 25-year-old gay male holding his orange scarf like a security blanket.

I ended up staying on my friend's couch until I moved to Pittsburgh to start my life over (again). All sorts of emotions ran through my system like guilt for defending myself, shame for having such a fearful family, gratitude for thinking ahead to make friends inside my essential oil network and radical faith in believing everything is going to be okay. Or as the beautiful Marie Forleo says "Everything is figureoutable."

Marie's life and business coach words gave me the immunity I needed to figure out my life and not let the illusions of police or family to define my worth or confidence in humanity. It was also this magical orange scarf that pulled me back to the light when I found myself drifting to that all familiar shame corner where my inner child doubted his existence.

If my orange scarf could knit confidence back into my 16-year-old self then I knew it would encourage my 25-year-old self to live life fearlessly. Orange juices my craft and my purpose on this planet to stay vivaciously alive. And continue to reach out to people and organizations that care to make a difference. Because that's what I learned the most. I'm alive and that's more than enough to keep me fired up and ready to go for lifetimes to come.

Yes, that's my orange scarf you see as my altar cloth. It's swirls remind me that we create our own karma and like my mom says, what goes around comes around. Orange is the embodiment of the energy I generously give to the world. I must create. I have no choice but to completely and joyfully co-create with the divine source of all. Building this altar helped me heal my relationship with justice. That truly it's not my place to seek out vengeance on humanity because the Universe has checks and balances already in place. Perhaps this is why you see those Buddhist monks rocking their orange like nobody's business. It's a very holy color. I find a great happiness in the color orange.

It feels like home to me.

I USED MY IMAGINATION TO MAKE THE GRASS WHATEVER COLOR I WANTED IT TO BE

WHOOPI GOLDBERG

The Power of Yellow

The color yellow empowers the solar plexus chakra. Here we move out of our creative wild animal instincts and start making our way up the yellow brick road befriending our body and mind connection through valuing self-esteem and altruism. This is the first color evolution in attempt to cultivate reason and highlights discernment in order to innovate our well-being. Recognizing that our consciousness filters our reality.

We can choose to live like a wounded captive by our predetermined heredity and early childhood conditioning or we can surrender to a sense of free-will and challenge our sense of well-being beyond our family's limitations, saying yes (or no) more frequently to secure boundaries or simply live with more gratitude and appreciation. Yellow energy strengthens our ability to digest the good, bad and ugly parts of life and shifts our focus on positivity. Like the saying goes, what you choose to focus on grows. It's this potent concentration that determines your reality and beliefs. Breaking down what we've been served and being able to extract value from life takes deliberate and persistent practice.

Yellow is a bright color of happiness but it's also about intellectualizing the world around you. I've studied positive psychology and I teach others to make the distinction that everyone has an individual happiness set point. As we experience the good, bad or ugly that luminous pendulum swings back to your subjective happy place. Esteem and community service shifts this happy meter. When I was unemployed, I stopped focusing on what I didn't have and completed a mini color reading for myself.

One of the colors that came forward in this three-card draw was firefly yellow. It's this energy that motivated me to put on some lemon essential oil in my cold-air diffuser, clean up the clutter in my space and decide to volunteer my time at the local Gay and Lesbian community center. By tapping into this personal power, I innovated my mind and to shine by example for others to take control in how they respond to their circumstance. Everything is not as it appears to be when you have the lights off.

Because of using yellow proactively, I altered my reality and perception of my conditions. Accessing abundance I couldn't see before because my ego wanted to stew in misery instead of choosing a much less resistant pathway.

My altruistic attitude supported my mood and it helped me get over the selfishness of living in scarcity and more centered in the abundance of service and community building. What we choose to say, think or even feel conditions our belief systems and ultimately our perceptions about the world's wellness and our own happiness.

If you're constantly in survival mode, you're truly less likely and more closed off to feeling a deep sense of personal fulfillment. Money and material objects do sustain your personal happiness but only after a certain peak after which feeling purposeful and happy depends on making the proper connections and serving the greater good.

Harvesting happiness overtime grows exponentially as you choose to stand tall like a giant sunflower following the path of light daily. I'm learning to live on this renewable positive energy to properly weed out the toxins in my life. And distill the best moments that life has to graciously gift to me and others I meet on this yellow brick path.

After my frightening escape from the wicked witch and her flying monkeys (aka being evicted and having to go to court), I found myself standing on a yellow bridge in Pittsburgh, Pennsylvania. The city of black and yellow became my new home as I learned how to rebalance my relationship with the world. I stopped on the Andy Warhol bridge and faced the sun affirming my gratitude and power.

I am love, I am light, I am color and I am home.

It was the last word home that pushed me over the edge of joy. I had an a-ha moment. Home doesn't have to be a physical location dictated by family. It's a feeling of peace and self-assurance. Home is what I feel in response to love, light and color. And because of this homecoming, I lean into my faith everyday now more aggressively. Obnoxiously positive despite criticism and contempt. I felt the sunlight burn through my aura and offer me a brand new life to wear. Like how Gandalf the Grey resurrected from the hell fires and became Gandalf the White. Or how a lump of coal transforms into a diamond. This is my white hot truth.

In those summer weeks after moving to Pittsburgh, I found a temporary job (a major shift in using positive thinking), I got my very first apartment and I knew that in order to cleanse my energy after such ridiculous drama, I decided to take care of my holistic (body, mind and soul) wellness by eating mindfully, using less chemicals and being deliberate with my personal finances. Living chemical-free and managing your money is easy once you commit to the light. And having a cleaner relationship to my body and mind in these ways opened up a greater field of purpose and prosperity.

If I hadn't been forced to fly away from the witch's castle, I'd be living in complete darkness not seeing my own happiness and self-worth. Pretending poverty and pain is all there is in the world. I wake up every day now holding deep positivity about my past and potential future. My happiness set point certainly shifted because I can feel my instincts sharpened and I have others telling me how much I light up their world like a firefly. It's called bioluminescence baby!

I've been more conscious of my consumerism now that I'm living on my own. Yeah, I don't have the deepest pockets and I don't need super billions. But I have a brain, a heart and a whole lot of courage as you might have already noticed. I enjoy tracking my spending and highlight key budgets for my business. One of the main distractions in living well and happy is this elusive element in our dimension called money. And I'm not a financial expert by any means but the *DebtFreeGuys* I follow online have taught me so much in their blog posts and podcasts on financial freedom. I know that money and debt can be hard to digest especially for someone like me who comes from a family that lives on government aid. I know assistance ain't bad, but it is a very abused system. I've learned it's empowering to make your own money. Everyone's situation is unique and I'm offering a colorful perspective on living prosperous in body, mind and soul so that you can create a positive relationship with abundance. Not feel overly attached to handouts that you never experience the power of your own financial integrity.

The power of yellow translates not only in mastering money, but eating, cleaning and highlighting the care for your space with pure intention. I love being able to eat healthy. Because then my brain and gut can enjoy munching on real power. And I've noticed my feelings and emotions are balanced. Helping me make friendlier buying decisions. One thing I learned living with other impoverished people is that we make some very poor financial decisions because we can't think or feel clearly because we're too busy stuffing our faces with junk that's keeping the lights off both figuratively and literally.

Today, I'm taking steps to restore my relationship with food. I have bananas, yellow apples and golden pears regularly. And as the Divine loves to put people on our path for a reason, I started following Dr. David Perlmutter who is all about food being a source of information for your body. Naturally, you want to make sure you consider the source of what you put inside your body and what you use in your personal space. We end up misjudging crucial life decisions and choices because of having a poor diet which sabotages our energy and emotions. This is why in color readings I inform people about consulting with a qualified nutritionist to balance their alkaline and acidic levels through a natural detox or develop a food plan that attunes them to eating more color every day. Colorful rainbow plates of real food - yum! And if you need inspiration, look on *Instagram* there are a ton of proper food junkies to follow! The bland colorless food you're eating could be the biggest factor in blocking your personal happiness and abundance!

Let's shine light on your living expenses so that you're aware of a cleaner way to live that feels bright and serves the greater good at the same time! The last way I love to use the power of yellow is in how I clean my apartment. I'm super proud to contribute to our beloved human civilization by using the plant-based cleaning products through my essential oil company. I have the company's all-purpose cleaner, dish soap, hand soap and of course using essential oils like lemon is great for different do-it-yourself projects to make sure me and my apartment's energy is bright-ass-warrior clean. That's the power of essential oils, baby!

I wouldn't be mentioning this to you if I knew it didn't work. What makes this legitimate for me is the company's integrity to sourcing, taking care of the planet through innovative stewardship (pesticide free farming – oh baby), community restoration projects all over Mama Earth and the loyalty program in place so that I get up to 25% cashback in product points so all my cleaning, essential oils and personal care is chemical-free and comes from a conscious company. Easy steps I take to live light.

It's seriously the best part of my life because I wouldn't be here living on my own and making the world a better place. Another win for altruism! I enjoy streamlining my products and essential oils because it would be expensive as fuck sending all my money to shady companies that don't essentially give back to it's community or the world in kind. This is a brilliant way to live happy and lighten up my finances through simple and sustainable proactive income. Because there's nothing passive about true prosperity.

Innovating our economy and supporting our friends and small businesses makes the world feel purposeful and enlightening. I encourage you to live chemical-free as best you can and set the intention to get rid of serious toxins. You can download the *ThinkDirty* app on your phone to go through your cabinets and throw away very harmful chemicals. And make the switch to using plant-based products and sign up for essential oils that make a difference.

As for my altar, the apple says it all.

Positive spirit is Mother Nature's currency for true abundance, wellness and the pursuit of happiness. And having this knowledge is power.

I MADE A CIRCLE WITH A SMILE FOR A MOUTH ON YELLOW PAPER BECAUSE IT WAS SUNSHINY AND BRIGHT

HARVEY BALL

THE POWER OF GREEN AND PINK

In my color practice, I assign the heart chakra both green and pink. Primarily, because this is how I perceive love and my own personal development. I also attribute these energies to how we embrace love as an extrovert or introvert. Are you pursuing love actively and draw that love from the outside, or are you allowing love passively to grow inside of you and internalize self-compassion? Of course, there are many degrees and variance in our color spectrum as life naturally swings in favor of diversity, so I encourage you to keep pursuing both masculine and feminine ways to learn, grow and evolve as a mindful being on this sacred planet. Versatility flexes muscle and heart.

Love is most certainly a never-ending classroom. And seeing love in these colors help me to mindfully stay present to the beauty of the process. After I graduated college in December 2012, I moved back home to live with family and started talking to a Libra guy who graduated the same time but at a different university. He moved back home and we met through *OkCupid*.

Meeting people online is second nature for me as I have a monogamous marriage with the digital age. It's through experiencing all of my romance and relationships, that I began to figure out and formulate my personal style of love. It's not always a definitively clean path to figuring out how relationships work or what needs to be present to cultivate a hearty crop because all parties involved in the process just aren't the same with each life moment/interaction/conversation and must be open to practicing self-awareness and self-compassion. *Did you hear me?* Open! Not closed off thinking assuming this is all you are or how everyone in the world is a revision of your ex or past circumstances. You never had this exact experience with this exact person wearing those exact clothes on this exact day. Love evolves. Each day is a new day to see yourself, your partner and the world with fresh new eyes.

I'm one of those people that you'll find in the self-help section not because I'm too broke from my past or obsessed with finding the right person for me. I'm there because I realize that broken crayons really do keep coloring and that the right person to love first is always and will be - me. How else do I save others if I can't save myself first? It's my lifelong curiosity to learn and expand on how to grow my mind and heart. Flexing those heart and soul muscles don't make you less desirable because you value improvements or weaker of a person because you enjoy focusing on that deeper first-hand magic. You are so brave going on this journey with me. In my personal observations, I see people every now and again make no effort to transform their stubbornness and welcome a better version of themselves or how they live life. It's the daily and ordinary habits that reinforce our limits. If you think you can't or can, you're right but don't complain when life forces you to grow and adapt.

It's like when my mom avoids upgrading her phone's software. Eventually, all the apps stop working, phone speed slows down, battery loses juice faster and the storage pop-up keeps reminding her that she's hanging onto the past for too long. She texts me about it. I ask if she upgraded her phone. No. Well, how do you expect your phone to love you if you don't love it and press that upgrade button. I see friends and relatives all the time settle for poor quality toxic conditions and too afraid to face their fears. Taking life in your own hands in order to make something meaningful scares the shit out of some people. It's this laziness that keeps you small. I see it happen with my clients that don't use enough color to evolve their own love. They fear being different. Scoffing at younger versions of themselves for not knowing enough, expressing too much and loving the world too quickly. Arrogantly adulting themselves to death.

Showing yourself very little self-compassion isn't a kind of reward for being a resilient muscle-minded grown up. If anything you're holding yourself hostage like a parent who emotionally and verbally abuses the child. You don't get a special grown-up sticker for giving yourself a hard time when you gossip about your troubles with other grown-ups. Pillaging love's purpose is a punishment and millions of people do it subconsciously every single day because we're out of balance with the heart chakra.

Coddling procrastination isn't good for personal development and growth either. So there are times for tough love which are moments when your soul wears a hardhat while it runs around with blueprints and maps out your construction site. Wondering what you're building? Your own legacy. And what better way than to build it with love. It's this fortitude and stewardship of self-discovery that saturates life with loads of more love. You are a living legacy of real pure love.

Usually, we just follow suit from our parents. And as a child of divorce and abuse, I know more about what not to do then what to do when it comes to love. Until I discovered that Gary Chapman wrote this insightful book called *The 5 Love Languages.* When I took the test to discover how I attune and attain love it was very enlightening as I've always given and actively expressed my love through spending quality time with people. And how I prefer to take or passively receive love is through encouragement and physical touch! This is what the heart chakra energy is all about. Proactively exchanging love with yourself and others.

Alas this was all hindsight to me, but for you may it be foresight. In February 2013 BCM (before color mage) for Valentine's Day weekend, I decided to hop on a bus and surprise my newfound beloved I met on *OkCupid.* It's in my Aries nature to be impulsively passionate. I took a bus on a whim of the heart and followed where Goddess Isis would send me. Hoping to reunite with my own Osiris. I arrived in the city and met that Libra guy for the first time. The moment was full of flutters and glitter. The usual love and bubbles carried us away. Since we've been talking for months, we did decide to make the relationship official. I returned home with a fancy boyfriend title to my name and at the same time dived into Gabrielle Bernstein's *May Cause Miracles* book. It's this journey that opened my eyes to self-love. And while I asked for miracles, I intuitively surrounded myself with the power of green and pink. I chose to wear more green, drink green tea, and meditate holding my rose quartz crystals over my chest as opened myself up more to the Divine. Secretly, I wanted this new relationship and this miracle journey to wake me up.

And oh it did!

When I mentioned what I was doing with most of my time, my Libra boyfriend had very little acceptance of my path. He struggled to wrap his journalistic brain around my inspirations. He mocked my card readings, intuitive strength and spirit junkie practice. He referred to my soul path as childish and immature. At the same time, I pursued finding a postgraduate job but no bites. I didn't feel as excited as I did with following this miracle journey. Something about it made me feel alive and full. Like I had a purpose greater than myself to make a real difference in the world.

Despite the staunch rejection, I continued to follow through with my videos and blogging. Even on days, when he came to visit me, I was committed to the divine and healing myself. Our long distance relationship was financially and emotionally taxing but it would become one of those miracle moments that would teach me to lean into self-compassion and love myself regardless of the cynical and jaded individuals to afraid to love with a heavy dose of real magic.

By the grace of some higher power, I received a chance to interview for a health insurance company as a social media manager. I felt confident with the position and thought the interview went well. But because I didn't relay the interview news to my boyfriend until after the fact, he got mad. I scheduled and rescheduled for a second interview but the timing was bad for the employer. And eventually I took the hint and at the same time, there was an eclipse that weekend. Eclipses typically are the energetic equivalent to going into a home and exterminating the cockroaches. That's what the Universe did for me with all this extraneous debris piling up in my soul house. I was hoarding negative energy and it wasn't helping my purpose. Naively accepting guilt and shame about developing my soul makes no sense. So if anyone tells you that your personal development is not necessary or isn't a priority. Don't fucking listen.

I made the decision that eclipse weekend to let the divine take over. I didn't try to save the relationship when I was threatened with an ultimatum and I didn't desperately follow up with the employer giving me the runaround. I chose self-compassion over compulsion. Over a fight via text, my ex told me that I lacked compassion and he was right. Compassion for myself. I didn't fully realize this because I've been so conditioned to play certain roles that brainwash you into trying to please everyone but yourself. Just because I'm positive and a free-spirit doesn't mean I sacrifice how I feel for the sake of sucking off someone's ego.

That summer I didn't wallow in guilt or shame about my raw personality. I don't feign what my heart feels or doesn't feel. I retaliated the best way I knew how, personally develop a deeper understanding of compassion. So I went to the library and checked out Karen Armstrong's book *Twelve Steps to a Compassionate Life* after I finished *May Cause Miracles*. Karen's book gave me a tremendous amount of light and love about how I should adult in this world. Thoughts I should play on repeat inside my head to let my heart take the lead. And it's this bounce back attitude that constructed the gateway to pursuing my color practice full time. I declared to the universe that I will serve love, light and color to the world and that's what I've been doing for almost half a decade. And if that wasn't enough confirmation, I found an adorable green caterpillar that same day climbing a beautiful rhododendron. Color guides us to be the teacher and the student in dark times.

Sitting on my green and pink altar is *May Cause Miracles*. And although the making of this altar would take place more than a year after the break up, I'm delighted to retrace my steps and include it's presence in my space to remind me of the tough love I needed to rebuild myself. You'll feel a certain power going through your own belongings to place together with intention. Adding plants to this specific altar grows the vibration of love and stronger compassion for the Earth. As you take care of the plant, you take care of yourself. Same happens when you devote yourself to personal development. Taking care of the divine inside you also takes care of the divine found all over the world. And wouldn't you know, taking care of the divine in the world, takes care of you in kind.

Speaking of kind, my favorite mantra from Gabby's book is "Kindness created me kind." I have it on a love note inside a special mojo self-love bag that I keep near me. Sometimes we forget to follow the magic and meaning of our own hearts because we become so obsessed with adulting other people's expectations. Pretending those expectations are our past, present and future. So using green and pink in your life helps you to follow a path to self-love. And build a new legacy out of the old and new love you carry into the future for yourself and the world.

With color one obtains an energy that seems to stem from witchcraft

Henri Matisse

THE POWER OF BLUE

The color blue leads the throat chakra. Flowing out of the Middle Earth energy of the heart as we begin to speak up for ourselves and advocate autonomy. Blue is a common color for building trust and many social media platforms use this color to create a more polite and vocal atmosphere. Social media is also founded on the notion that everyone is entitled to free speech and expression as long as it's not harming or inciting action that breaks the law. Thumbs up.

My blue journey has two parts to reflect on how my leadership evolved since living more in sync with the power of color. To start, I participated in other high school organizations besides art. I'm multi-passionate so I often completed

61

community service projects, wrote human rights letters, and acted in the school's rendition of *The Sound of Music*. On top of my extracurricular involvements, I was inspired to believe in myself even more by wanting to become a television talk show host like Ellen DeGeneres. I would just stare into her show's sky blue color and it inspired me with this crazy idea that I could do what she's doing. It got me thinking, that everything I see around me is connected to a job or a dream. Seeing her advocate herself to the world through her own voice and build a platform on love, kindness and laughter made me feel the power of empathy and soul truth. I want that kind of impact. I want to be felt, seen and recognized as a lighthouse in this world. I want others to see me for me.

It was throughout high school, I told everyone my dream. But something scratched louder at the door when it comes to speaking my truth with the world. I had already accepted myself being gay. And I mentioned it to my classmates. Collecting those rainbow brownie points baby was easy with my orange scarf but also because enrolling in a private boarding school for kids coming from low-income families and rough backgrounds, humbled our humanity for one another. It's amazing when you just give children an opportunity to love without labels.

Although the news of my sexuality went around the campus like wildfire (a perk of being outspoken), my next hurdle was to enhance respect for myself by telling the school administration. Gulp. Authorities.

One of the biggest regrets I have about high school is not being able to start and sustain a Gay and Straight Alliance at the school. I did bring it up on multiple occasions and many adults told me that it goes against the foundational beliefs of the school. When staff told me that lame ass excuse, I rebelled. It wasn't an effective way to make progress. Advocating for one's self takes grace and skill. At this point in my life, I'm a piss ant sticking it to the man. But no one pays attention or listens to you when you're so focused on the conspiracy and less on the change you seek.

Eventually, I accepted that I wasted time complaining about the system and policies and set the intention to right my wrongs in a better light.

It's a requirement that all graduating seniors give a final presentation to the senior staff to showcase what we've learned over the past four years as a student and aspire to accomplish in our post graduate lives. This was my chance to be the leader I knew I wanted to be. I picked a spiritually sounding time slot (7 P.M. on the dot) and prepared the best way I knew how – color. I made sure my presentation was eye-catching. Direct. Bold. And spoke to my true colors. I put on my best suit with a blue pattern tie and walked with pride to give the most vulnerable presentation of my life. In front of a group of people I never met before, but apparently they would already know me from the school records.

The school keeps track of your academic and behavioral histories, so I knew these people knew very little about my real character. Come on, detentions and some sassy progress report points on a piece of paper doesn't define someone's soul. Absurd. So, I set the intention to distract them from the shadows of my past and take time to honor the light of my future. Autonomy expresses magic and encourages reconciliations to regenerate one's community.

When I entered the room, I could feel the sweat dripping from my arms and my tie felt snug on my throat. I could hear my voice crack when I introduced myself.

Uh hello. Thank you for being here with me. My name is Bernard and I am Gay. Over the course of my time here...

My voice trailed off as I began to occupy a different time and space. I felt my body give way to some force greater than myself and I just soaked in its power and authority. I let this being from another part of me take charge and click through my PowerPoint slides. Towards the end, I came back to my-self. And saw that the presentation was over. I stared at the surprised look on their faces and glanced at the screen. I saw a picture of Ellen Degeneres smiling at me and a rain-bow cutting through the school's logo. My senior presentation was a visual act of expression and edge. Graceful defiance. A bold statement of owning my authority. Because I'm not here to be tolerated. I'm here to feel understood, heard and above all respected as an individual. It's through creating, writing and showing up in my truth that I felt extraordinary. This presentation shifted my presence and pulled me closer to my power.

Taking one more look around, I asked if anyone had any questions. A vaguely familiar gentleman I saw in school pam-phlets chimed in and explained to the room he didn't have a question. But to share his remarks about the amount of lead-ership, strength and integrity it took to stand before people I never met and share myself in such a powerful way.

"You're the only one Bernard of your graduating class that I really do believe will make a difference in this world."

His words and expression articulated angelical communication. As if all the struggle and resistance had a purpose leading me to this very moment in my young adult life. A foreshadowing of greatness and impact that later would enrich my color mage practice. To have an authority figure express respect and listen to me from a place of empathy inspired me to feel better about the state of the school and the world.

He did have one critique about my presentation, pulled me to the side just before I left the room and told me that I was wearing too much cologne. So, I just bobbed my head in compliance and changed the subject, "Oh, what a nice blue tie you have on."

My leadership after high school grew as I became the President of my university's chapter of *National Broadcasting Society* and traveled abroad to Scotland to complete an international social media internship. After I graduated from college, I decided to volunteer for *Equality Pennsylvania.* And it was my job to go around to small business owners and ask for their support against LGBT discrimination. One day, I spent 5 gaily forward hours cruising local businesses weeks before Pennsylvania passed same-sex marriage.

In my canvassing, I found many business owners avoided making a choice. Most people preferred to be left alone. To cynical in taking a stance out of fear. They felt insignificant. And this bystander effect I learned in my high school street law class, serves no one but the timid. People who struggle

with the color blue or the throat chakra are fearful of responsibility and acting upon their own authority. Expecting someone else to take care of their support. This lack of involve-
ment and advocacy stagnates progress and clouds authenticity. If you require change, you better believe that it's not
going to come from pretending the world is going to fix itself.
It's the grassroots foundation from the heart chakra that
gives you a place to have your blue book opinions.

After moving to Pittsburgh, I rallied with thousands of parents, children and advocates during the largest most powerful Women's March in 2017. I saw a sea of sassy magenta
pink hats and I decided to wear my 80s dragon green blazer
to balance the heart chakra vibes. Inside my pocket, I carried
an evil eye to ward off ill-intent or evil. I set the intention that
we have a right to be here. Advocating for rights that most
enjoy, but too scared to act on and defend. You can see my
evil eye talisman on my altar space that I carried during the
rally.

Also on my blue altar, I have blue candles lit because some
LGBT youth were being mistreated from what I saw in the
news while I was coloring my space that week. As a way to
pray and meditate using the power of blue, I invoked the angels to guide and guard my soul family. Blue needs to be
part of the media because all that red incites too much violence and hatred like a rabid fox infecting the world with sen-
sational click bait tactics. Yuck. So I counter the energy with
blue to encourage balance and trust that authorities in
charge are doing an honest transparent job.

If you discover people in your life disrespecting you or you
feel yourself lacking the inspiration to live authentically use
blue to energize your power to be heard and pray to

Archangel Michael to deliver protection in your community. It takes bravery to speak the truth and stand for what you believe in despite lower vibrational opinions one encounters through angry news or extreme authoritarian hate speech. By expressing your essence, you declare integrity and it makes it so much easier to communicate and tap into the language of your true colors.

It's okay to shine out of the blue, uninvited.

This is a revolutionary way to color our life especially as we restore faith and peace in the Trump era. I firmly believe that coloring our life with stronger intentions and stepping into our leadership is knocking down walls and building rainbow bridges all over the globe. A big kind of magic is already here. And it starts with you using the power of color to change your mood and mindset about expressing real truths. Holding self-respect. And regenerating your community, team and soul family to encourage liberty and life for all.

THE EXPRESSION OF BEAUTY IS IN DIRECT RATIO TO THE POWER OF CONCEPTION THE ARTIST HAS ACQUIRED

GUSTAVE COURBET

THE POWER OF PURPLE

The color purple sees beyond the surface of the third eye chakra. This is the Oprah of your chakra system. You want to feel that super mega empire self then this is where most spiritually inclined folks choose to hang and mastermind with the Divine. Purple has been a highly sought after color throughout the ages because of it's cultural implications of social status and mastery in obtaining divine wisdom.

The pineal gland is often referred to as the physical location of one's third eye. Rene Descartes once said that the pineal gland is *the seat of the soul.* Although I'm not too certain your soul only lives in this small headspace, I do find this energy center magical and equally mysterious. While building my purple altar, I noticed it was unlike my previous altars because this was the one color I lacked the most in my space, but assumed would be the easiest considering my spiritual nature. I felt like a fraud. Not much was going on. I was shocked. I reflected for hours trying to make out what this exactly meant for my journey.

Does this mean I'm doing all this intuitive magic stuff but secretly not understanding the real power of purple? Am I less of a wizard and more of a con artist?

And so I got serious with the color purple to figure out what I would later discover as my impostor syndrome. The impostor syndrome is a complex that my friend Tanya Geisler, life and business coach rips into step-by-step with her TED talk on claiming that awesome seat at the head of the table ...authority. Turns out that we all go through this at different times in our lives and it makes us feel like we're all alone in the world. Invisible and that our dreams or expertise is only an illusion. This deception felt real as I looked at my purple altar. Then I had this notion to stop wallowing over the lack and actually use this moment to practice what I preach. It became a livable moment for me to use color to change my life once again.

Coloring my hair purple was a delicious wild step. It went against my childhood rules and it definitely told potential employers who looked at my online photos to not hire me because I don't listen to conformity very well. I had to follow my intuition and completely own the fact that I'm living proof of the power of color. The transformation happened shortly after joining my essential oil company because I started using oils specifically to broaden my color therapy expertise and support my personal vision quests during meditations. It was my friend who introduced me to the oils who also owned a hair salon. And I decided to go to her as a professional to take care of my hair color because I wanted to experience the presence of a real authority. No more box color for me, that day I vowed to go pro with my beauty. I put faith in the technology and alchemy that went into my hair transformation. Taking this step also transformed my relationship to financial security (trusting that my hair color would build brand awareness and that means more sales) and feeling more true to my spiritual path of color.

While I sipped on hot lavender tea, my eyes avoided looking at the mirror so I could absorb my new identity once the cut and color was finished. Euphoria grew inside me as my friend detangled some loose strands of fear I had about taking care of my beauty and feeling empowered about how I wanted to be seen in the world.

I'll appear more feminine to the world, but should I care? I find it interesting how my personal aura is so adaptable and it shapeshifts so beautifully between worlds. I can be as masculine or as feminine as I'd like to be since I'm just being myself. Soul not only bends space and time but gender as well. I embrace my magic over the monotonous myths society chooses to distract us with any day.

Changing my hair color was a personal uprising to raise the vibration in the world and see life in a new way. When my friend swirled my chair around to face the mirror, I couldn't stop looking at my eyes. I swelled up in tears. I felt the person who was trapped inside me for all those years was finally set free. Like a butterfly coming out of its chrysalis, I was ready to use my wings.

Contrary to me growing up bullied by adults and kids, I wasn't made fun of because of my new hair. No one ever came up to me and questioned my decision. I walked in public stronger and taller. This presence was my power and I used color to get me here. People complimented me out of nowhere and this only reminded me that the Divine sees me. Sees how I'm being brave on this planet and wanted me to know through the kindness of those walking nearby that beauty is real and it's seen.

Of course, I do believe miserable jealous people attempted to throw shade (I'm far from naïve) but those dark tendrils of hate never pierced my perception. If there were insults or objections, I didn't know because the malice couldn't even reach me energetically as my indigo personality was just too prestigious to let someone else's ego influence my authentic beauty.

Over the months, the color morphed from lilac lavender to a deep pungent magenta that enriched my expertise and public relations. It's this deep juicy ombre luxury that carried an interstellar presence and gave me the clarity around my brand and ultimately getting published on *Positively Positive*. An online space for positive inspiration and features prominent thought leaders like Danielle LaPorte, Gabrielle Bernstein and Pencils of Promise founder, Adam Braun. So, to have been seen among such lighthouses was an immense honor. Leveraging my spiritual journey in this way offered my expertise to help others feel the power of owning their own transformations using color.

Besides my hair changing my perspective, I was adamant about living independent and getting my own place that I started researching intense crystals not your typical generic recommendations to support what I had on my vision board and make it a reality. Now, I'm certified in law of attraction, neurolingustic programming and of course color so I naturally had a good bucket of tools to use. But I felt that calling like I normally would when the Divine wanted something more from me. I had the tug and pull of my intuition to purchase something with prestige in order to make shift happen. And in a couple of days I found a purple crystal called charoite. And I have that as a necklace to spearhead my visions.

When manifesting it's far better to have clarity because that means you have more insight into the specific power and resonance that ultimately drives and influences your manifestations. Building my beliefs about money, power and getting my own space changed as a result of investing in my personal and professional visions.

I used this crystal and purple to remind me of those groovy vibes that I want to feel as magical misfit in this world. This particular crystal invokes independence relating well with one of the cards in traditional tarot – the chariot. Usually the traditional art for the card features a white and black element and this represents the duality between light and dark. You need this yin and yang balance to move through intuition, synchronicity and prayer for the highest good.

Even using this crystal while I scrolled through my Facebook newsfeed helped me see how others fall off their proverbial chariots all the time on social media or in real life by trying to grab everyone else's riches by comparing their journey and trying to imitate the successes (or intuition) of their friends, family and competition.

Focus is the key to avoid falling victim to feeling like a fraud. I learned to live independent from the amateurs and resistant to my rivals. Purple helped me to learn that dirty impostors bootleg intuition. Authorities inspire intuition.

Through all the purifying and clarity cleansing I've been through I'm finally living on my own – a win for perseverance! Personal independence is still new to me as I'm always learning to see the world with new eyes. Envisioning a plan and path equipped through color, I mastermind with friends and clients on making their manifestations real.

On my purple altar, I have a deck of cards layered across my altar space because I see intuition expanding all over the world as we see ourselves leveraging our intuitive authority instead of imitating it. I would have used my color deck but that came after I did this color revolution for myself. Even though there was a lack of purple, I was proactive in taking this journey deeper. I feel free from the distractions of fear. Having faith in metaphysical practices to attract physical out-comes. Becoming flexible with our emotional connections to our life stories. Using our wisdom and foresight to envision a brighter future. Giving ourselves the permission to raise vi-bration and listen openly to intuition.

After building my altar, I placed more value in clairvoyance, intuitive liberties and faith outside of political or religious dogma so that the Divine could continue to help me see beauty and assist others like yourself to overcome the myth. I think this is what Alice Walker meant when she said,

"I think it pisses God off if you walk by the color purple in a field somewhere and don't notice it. People think pleasing God is all God cares about. But any fool living in the world can see it always trying to please us back."

Whether it's God, Goddess or the Universe, it's watching. Living this life with you, as you and through you. Seeing your real beauty despite physical appearances. Yes, changing outer appearances can help validate and affirm what you feel inside, but it's not a requirement to live and feel independent. Have faith in your own gospel of truth and don't feel the pressure to imitate anyone because absolutely no one is you.

I FOCUS A LOT ON MY VOICE BECAUSE I WANT IT TO BE AN INSTRUMENT AS WELL I WANT MY VOICE TO ADD COLOR

THEOPHILUS LONDON

THE POWER OF WHITE AND METALLIC

The color white (if you choose metallic also) vibrates ascension in the crown chakra. White connections include marriage, death and angels. It's this higher chakra that holds your higher self. A version of the real you that has access to quantum powers of timelessness, agelessness, gracefulness and innocence. Complete freedom. An open canvas to play in the field of possibility and light. Liberation from chains that attempt to limit your peaceful presence. The source of light that sees all, knows all and connects with all from an opalescent throne shining from the crown center. And it's here where you journey to experience emergence, peace and surrender into oneness. No more living separate in religion, race or region.

You are one. We are one. They are one. All are one. One energy married to the Divine light of all existence. Surrender to this truth. Let go of your fear and dark borders that manipulate you. Give up the apathetic aristocracy.

Welcome yourself home.

Growing up, my grandmother would babysit my siblings and I while our mom was out working or getting food for the family. It's also when I rebelled against the hand that fed me. Giving my grandmother a hard time. Looking down at her in my early years, because I accepted her place according to how others treated and looked at her. Positioning her in a corner to play the black sheep of the family. The crazy lady who lived in the projects. She also was obsessed with collecting angel figurines, rummaging through yard sales, and always needing the latest *Women's World* magazine. It wasn't until I was forced to live with her one summer in 2005 that I learned a valuable lesson about people. Eventually, the world.

After my mom divorced my father, we moved to a public housing development. The projects are simple apartments given to people in need of a space to live. If those white walls could talk, you'd find yourself hopeless with the world, because some of the residents live in very dark mindsets and poor conditions. Hooked up on drugs and violence. Abusing one another through gossip and celebrating their impoverished struggles with pride. I began believing that people with normal homes, rich families and popularity were all better than what I've been given. I thought those people who lived a completely different life than me were blessed by God's hands more frequently. Now, I know this is a major lie we tell ourselves out of pity and laziness but back then that's how my immature child logic made it out to be and I blindly believed in the deception. Rejecting my good nature, I took whatever frustrations I had and forced the burden on my grandmother. Feeling since she was poor and not working then it's her fault why we were living here in the first place.

I was blaming my grandmother for why my parents were so unhappy. The younger me was trying to make things better, but ultimately made things so much harder. I appreciate the contrast, but boy, it's far easier to make peace than try and win the war.

Because living in the projects became too vindictive and heartless, we moved into (get ready) my mom's ex-boyfriend's mother's house (mouthful I know). Like all of my other experiences with change, there's a short opening where everyone is patient with one another, and life feels balanced and happy. It doesn't last forever. We human creatures come out of our honeymoon high and the real work happens. True colors float to the surface. That *we're all in this together* phase quickly faded and I picked up on it.

Being an empath and a highly-sensitive person, I began noticing subtle things shift. Energy levels and the excitement to see each other slipped away. Offers to go out and do things as a group stopped. Whispering in the back rooms caught my ears. Then there was the undertone of arrogance in conversation. Your choice of words and how it's delivered matters. Empaths are great body language interpreters because they have this superpower to sense deception behind diction. I can feel people's auras as my own. To be honest, it's a blessing and a bit of a curse. A power struggle formed as I found myself facing false promises and dirty lies from people who believe they can mold me and my family into their minions just because they took us in because we needed a place to stay. Um, as if I'm going to compromise the light by sweeping your darkness under the rug. There's no fucking way that's happening. I'm the type of person that demands integrity and transparency. I could smell the pretentious odor one gave off when we were in the room so I psychically and mentally tuned their energy out of my life. Hearing only white noise and never looking directly at their eyes, a tactic I learned while being harassed in school.

It bothered me deeply that this middle class family who has a college education, money and a real home began acting just as mean-spirited and spiteful like those people in government housing. This turned my *they all have it better and are more pure than me* thinking on its head. Between the unruly mockery from school bullies and the superficiality that slithered the halls at "home" (big fat air quotes), I became arrogantly defiant toward authorities that belittled my humanity and picked on my self-esteem by trying to control my spirit. Talks of placing me into police academy and getting involved with sports were tossed between the adults as a form of punishment for me being too feminine, sensitive and outspoken.

The summer before high school, the ticking bomb went off and I was kicked out of the house at 14 and I had no choice but to stay with my grandmother. Yup, the same woman who I mocked and fought against. She was the only person who could take me in and make me see she relates to being an outcast. As the tables turned, I felt what she had felt all her life. I listened to stories of her past and her hopes for the future. We went to church together. It was never at the same one either. She had friends in many places and that positive busy body glow about her Leo personality made going out and connecting with people, God and life fun. Something I

80

hadn't felt before – peace. No more protesting or fighting to protect myself.

Over the course of these outings I learned that there isn't one right religion. Every branch of religion is an attempt to define, connect and feel meaning. Unfortunately, we let our ego and fear dictate our lives. Forcing us to kill off peace. When I feel into color, I'm understanding that the spectrum comes from white light. I see humanity like a prism giving rise to languages, races, identities and religions. Evolving in a creative dance with a Divine collective that every soul on the planet contributes to consciously and subconsciously. Stealing fire. Expanding our limits. A rainbowlicious disbursement of the timeless, ageless, graceful and innocent source that we all have access to regardless of the illusions in how much money you have or don't have, the car you drive or where you live. Spirit or magic isn't something you buy. It's who you are. And between those hallelujah hymns and Sunday lunches, I learned we are God as well as the peace we must learn to keep on this beautiful planet.

It's through diversity and culture that reminds us of our spiritual journey as humans to live transparent and free of darkness. Build hope not poison our lives with fear or criticism. You deepen your path and purpose on this planet by unconditionally allowing yourself and others to feel love, light and color for the highest good. Be the lighthouse of peace so others can see your light guiding them home. It's that simple. Be love. Be light. And be colorful even if it goes against the dark gray rain cloud everyone seems to hang onto.

That summer, I didn't just learn to surrender to God in multiple denominations or come to accept the quirks of my grandmother's humanity but embrace hope. Defend diversity.

Nana collected white and silver angel statues for a deeper purpose beyond having a hobby. She always ordered new drapery sets for the kitchen window even if she had no company over to admire it. While rearranging her entourage of winged guardians, I asked why she ordered these every month and she told me that the angels brought her peace. I couldn't argue with that so I asked about the kitchen drapes thinking I'd one up her wisdom. She blurted a laugh.

Because white walls are too bare without color.

Her words still echo around me as I look at my own apartment's white walls. And the reason why I have so many oils, books and crystals is the same reason she collected so many angel wings and curtains. Tools like this bring peace and power to sustain light in dark times. Giving us a way to color our body, mind and soul using the rainbow. Touching us with that extra bit of hope.

Adding color to a blank boring canvas is more fulfilling and joyful. The rainbow has been a historical symbol for hope, happiness and inclusion. Rainbow means everyone. Every single soul on this planet stems from this light source. And it would be super ugly and boring if we all were exactly the same. It's the prismatic human element of religions, races and geographic regions that diversify our universal light. Our humanity is beautiful because of our color. And there's no one color that reigns over the other. The rainbow teaches us that together light is a bridge not a wall. And when we accept this truth, we find peace. And eventually we find our way home.

White allows me to uncover the ultimate unity I have with all of life beyond fear and condition. I'm not separate from my grandmother or the guy behind me at the grocery store. Because all color, all race and all spiritual soul paths all want to feel one thing – home.

My white altar was very humbling to piece together. I saw rainbows bounce into my bedroom from the metals I used. I felt the energy was porcelain but full of promise. I held each piece with reverence. I incorporated a white key to unlock my higher power, an elephant necklace that my grandmother gave me weeks before I started this altar journey and a quartz crown I created to cleanse my own crown chakra. I did make a honey pot ritual to include on the space because I wanted to purify and soothe all of the broken and burned out relationships in my life . And I wanted to start over and let go of anyone who wasn't meant to hang around forever.

Permission to surrender to a divine plan.

I included metallic energy like silver to remind myself of the persistence it takes to not only find hope, but reflect that hope in darkness. The death and beauty found in the dandelion starbursts reminded me of the fragility and vulnerability to believe in letting go of your seeds, ideas and hopes so that wisdom grows in the darkest cavities of our culture.

This final week allowed me to reflect greatly on invoking a greater sense of peace with life and death. Knowing that with absolute certainty that everything is working out. Should you fall victim to fear, ego or darkness please know that you are the love you seek, you are the light you want and you are the color after the storm.

We have to try, do and ultimately make any effort to open and surrender to that peace we all carry. May your own journey feel the power of your peaceful presence. Protection is best suited with light not war. Merge into your enemies and struggles by kissing forgiveness first. And don't forget to give your own white walls all the color you can muster.

And as for the angel who touched my life, Nana now has clouds for walls, rainbows for drapery and is home with her own tribe. She passed away months after I did this journey on Christmas Eve because of heart failure and never regaining mobility after her stroke in 2008. Looking back, I knew deep within my soul I needed to place that elephant necklace on my altar as a way to heal in advance. I wanted this to open more love and light in my corner of the sky, but this is about real magic and not limiting healing to just our own life. But to step deeper into the light, and heal those angels in our life that might not realize their own power yet. With good sweet intentions one may cast magic and prayer on behalf of the greater good. Just be sure to use white when you do.

Two week's before Christmas, I got a text telling me Nana wasn't doing so good so I went to see her while nurses and a social worker moved her into hospice care. I held her hand, talked to her with more presence and prayed silently she feels peace. My soul and her soul became one. I felt her body asking if it's okay to let go. I remember thinking to myself. Not now. You still have time.

All she could do was breathe heavy. And all I could do was be a good empath and healer massaging the light. Protecting the space around her aura. In stillness, I saw a white and silvery halo blanket across her tired body. Nana's eyes hinted toward a box with some of her belongings. Inside I spotted an angel and I asked if I could have it. A smile slipped from the corner of her mouth. She even gave me a sparkly black hat that was fun! Before leaving, I leaned close and told her I loved her to the moon and back. This was our favorite way to affirm our love. We started saying it that summer she took me in and have been wrapping our goodbyes with it ever since. Today, Nana lives peacefully inside a silver raindrop pendant next to her angel figurine in my sacred space. And I call on her when I need to be touched by an angel.

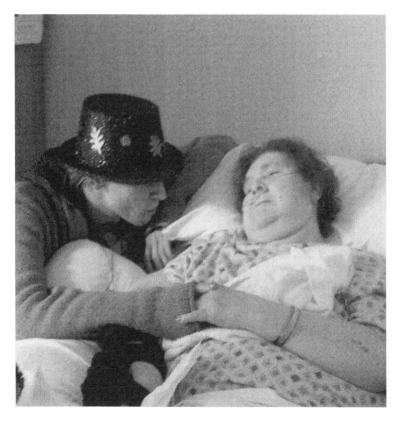

Nana and I. We sparkle.

NOW YOUR TURN TO PLAY WITH REAL MAGIC AND SPREAD YOUR WINGS

Beautiful sweet soul. Thank you for holding me close while we relived these moments together. Memories that highlighted scars, wounds, and phantoms of my journey. All of the energy work I've done using color in the last decade and all the life moments I wrestled with brought me to this point. There's nothing glamorous about this revolution. It takes participation, persistence and patience to shift moods and heal karma. I found that color is my favorite way to unblock resistance, create real change and be happy with myself even if it means ruffling a few feathers.

So what did I ultimately learn with each of the colors?

Red activates love at first sight. Orange braces my confidence. Yellow innovates how I detox money fears and happiness. Green and Pink develops self-love and compassion. Blue enhances equality. Purple leverages intuition. And lastly, white and metallic shines a light on unity and peace.

In the next part of the book, learn how to get your sparkle on by joining the rainbow revolution officially, polish your altar building skills with the five elements, and dive deeper into your own body, mind and soul using the journal prompts.

PART TWO
YOUR COLOR JOURNEY

I PREFER LIVING IN COLOR

DAVID HOCKNEY

JOIN THE REVOLUTION

I know how it's cool being the lone wolf. However, I wouldn't have gotten this far in my spiritual journey if it wasn't for being part of a movement. Finding your tribe is a revolutionary way to grow on your path. It's the people we meet that bring color to our world so we can leverage the power of love, light and color.

This is a personal and worldwide challenge to shift energy and bring the spectrum of humanity closer to our home and our heart. Stop defining your power based on outdated and broken systems. Our evolution as a species depends on how passionate, confident, innovative, compassionate, respectful, beautiful and peaceful you choose to be. Ingredients I had to discover and learn along the way through color. Very rarely does anyone need to be reminded of the war, grief and apathy already running loose in the world. Why not try something new. Build yourself a shrine of your power and commit to a revolutionary lifestyle. Clean space and hold energy that is chemical and toxin free.

The tasks are simple, yet life-changing. Should you choose to dedicate your energy to color for the next seven weeks, means you were born with this magic in your blood.

JOIN THE RAINBOW REVOLUTION
BOOK CLUB ONLINE

www.bit.ly/rainbowrevolution

CHALLENGE TIMELINE

Now it's your turn to put this journey to the test. For the next seven weeks, build your own altar following this process:

Week 1 – RED

Week 2 - ORANGE

Week 3 – YELLOW

Week 4 – GREEN AND PINK

Week 5 – BLUE

Week 6 – PURPLE

Week 7 – WHITE AND METALLIC

But remember you're not alone during this journey. Please share photos and videos of your color altars using the hashtag #rainbowaltar and #myaltar on social media so the world can feel your power.

This timeline is flexible, if you honestly want to spend more time and love with a particular color longer. Go ahead with your bad ass self. No one's looking. But remember the energy may collect some dust and you may get bored/numb to the juju. I don't want your passion to fizzle flat on the floor. So be open to riding this broomstick for as long as your soul requires. And if you happen to have a time turner, please share as I would love to use it to sprinkle a little more color in multiple places at once.

Five Elements You'll Need to Know to Build the Perfect Altar and Change the World

An altar has five elements you want to keep in mind: theme, location, decoration, upkeep and alterations. Each element will be personal and unique to you.

For each altar, be mindful to use all your senses: touch, taste, sight, sound, smell and even intuition through synchronicity. Expect your altars to inspire cheeky Universe moments. Sense subtle shifts, reconnections and new perceptions of your memories. Deeply connecting with your chosen objects by color allows your magic to shine strategically in your life.

Theme

Having an altar theme is super fun especially when you feel like you have the purpose to heal your sacred space. Many sample themes or altars go beyond beauty and capture moments of meditation, monthly goals, prayer/rituals, remembrance of loved ones who grew their own angel wings and seasonal tidings that the majority of people participate in the comfort of their own holiday celebrations. Decorating the home as the seasons change is a normal ritualistic experience that goes unnoticed if one is negligent about their living conditions. Being lazy while creating your altar influences the outcome of your manifestations. Keeping up with trends also tends to push the snooze button on creativity and real beauty. Why follow when you can lead a deeper relationship with your own space? Take your décor and objects used to build these altars seriously as you're adorning the soul of your heart and home.

For this challenge our theme is primarily color and you will build your own altars based on the colors of the rainbow and chakra spectrum: red, orange, yellow, green/pink, blue, purple and white/metallic. Giving you nine colors to work with over the seven weeks focuses your ability to connect and relate to your life in different areas without feeling like you're obligated to manifest every part of your reality all at once. No one has that power.

LOCATION

I don't expect you to keep your altars in one spot either. You should go ahead and move them if you feel called to set up in a different place over the weeks because I know energy moves and you may like your personal altar to do more than just act as a pile of unicorn poo poo. You may like it to generate energy and excite the room with a specific vibration. Part of the reason why I set my altars up in my bedroom was because it's my studio to film my color videos and make my magic happen. If I had a home to myself, I'd definitely sprinkle my color altars throughout the house. I see myself in the near future, building my green and pink altar in my bathroom. Practically I have the space to do so, but also, I want the self-compassion and growth to reflect back to me from the huge vanity mirror. On the downside, there's no window, so I don't think I'll keep any live plants in there. That's something to think about when deciding your location.

Usually people have a personal space (in the office, bedroom or perhaps a dedicated meditation studio) that they call their own and can set up their color altars and then rotate through the colors when the time comes. If you share a space with a lover, family or roomie, be mindful in allowing this to be a fun group effort instead of you hiding this juicy magic all to yourself. People are territorial creatures as I've learned so the more willing you are to include instead of exclude the happier the space will be for everyone! But you'll have to decide on this when it comes to picking the perfect place. The best part of what I do as a color reader is use my intuition and empathetic abilities to feel out spatial energy. Like how I naturally built my altar in the relationship corner, that's a win for intuition. Don't be afraid to connect.

My first job was being an apprentice for an interior design coordinator at my school. My favorite thing to do was create floral arrangements that paralleled the space's personality or theme. I would purposefully create pieces that reflected the vibration of the home. And if the arrangements were in high traffic areas like in the dining room or in the office, I infused my creations with powerful visual imagery. By projecting my energy into the object visualizing scenes of laughter or productivity (depending on the space's usage) I imbued it to energetically empower that space. Matching it with high vibes. Similar to how a Himalayan salt lamp floods the room with positive energy.

While building your altar, you want to match vibrations and feel your space come alive. Enjoy this process and don't for the love of God overthink this or you'll feel drained or fearful. As if you're doing magic wrong. You're not he-who-shall-not-be-named, so we're a far way from the dark arts. Allow your altar to pulsate and hum in harmony with the spot that feels most beneficial.

Color allows you to manipulate any space so that you can see and experience the energy an events you want. You want to focus on letting your imagination go wild with delight. Use the theme to inspire the positive images you want to happen inside this location that relate really well to each color. This challenge gives you practice to feel out the perfect room for your colorful altars by tuning into your own intuition. So use your imagination. Remember to not judge yourself when certain images and memories do surface. If you're struggling at any part of this experience, please reach out to me or the larger rainbow revolution community.

If you have pets, small children or arrogant people in your space, do be mindful that this highly focused attention draws energy. Your altars not only become a key focal point physically in the room, but also emotionally and spiritually. Since you're focusing on color instead of your traditional and timely (to be expected) holiday tidings, a space occupying specific color becomes attractive.

Touchy hands and amused personalities are destined to be curious about the powerful magic you're invoking. It's this different and eye-catching display that draws living energy closer to this area. Keep your altar out of reach of pets and children for safety reasons. If using candles be safe, read the labels and use proper judgment while handling with extreme care.

As for the curiously cynical that disapprove of your altar, don't pay them any attention and keep on coloring. Soon you'll have results and evidence to back up why you cast, conjure and create with your reality using color. You have the power to either feed into their disbelief and arrogance or you can choose to adorn their skepticism and spiritual apathy

with more light and more love. For every side-eye or cold re-
mark about this process, add even more color to your sacred
space and altars. Believe more in the process and you'll
breakthrough. Promise.

DECORATION

Speaking of candles....there are plenty of items to use to create beautiful eye popping and engaging altars that don't require an open flame. Let the items you choose speak to you
and your vision. Buying expensive figurines or crystals for
this journey are not the main focus in having the perfect altar.
Use what you have already around the home and if over the
course of the week, you notice that you need something extra or have to do something drastically meaningful to create
the shift you desire like changing your hair color then do it!

Color is an active vibration that insists you use it more in
your day to day adventures. I used what I had collected over
the years and objects that my ex might have touched or
seen. For my red altar, I used wooden roses that my ex and I
got when we went to the LGBT pride fest together. I felt
those were an essential part of my journey because I knew it
was a direct connection in starting the letting go process regardless of how cheap and flimsy it looks. An altar is always
best dressed with pure intention, love and resourcefulness.

However, if you tend to have a luxurious sweet tooth (no
shame) then you find what you can to make this journey feel
as authentic and powerful as you! I ended up for my green
and pink altar purchasing a local artist's painting. Something
about that juicy booty and temptress feeling resonated so
deeply with how I wanted to heal my heart chakra. The price

was a bit out there, but I take it as a way of investing in my wealth frequency as opposed to defaulting to my poverty mindset. Keep your financial integrity intact.

While decorating your altars, remember to bring your outside world inside when you're building with power. I'm always finding rocks, twigs and pinecones outside that I bring inside to enhance my space. Love, love, love pinecones by the way! There's a weeping willow branch on my green and pink altar. I have dried petals and even a few dandelions ready for wishes included in this experience as well. Having this connection with the natural world reminds me of my place here on the Earth. Use the juxtaposition between man-made objects and the real world to unearth a deeper meditative practice for transforming raw energy.

Last note, use your essential oil diffuser! I didn't get involved with essential oils until 2015. It's this color cleanse that opened my mind to new ways to add color and upgrade my life. It's by using oils now that's making all the difference in my world because I'm thinking in a completely different way about how I impact the world, improve my moods and re-shape my outlook about socioeconomic conditions. I'm more solution focused and less complaint driven. When I have my diffuser on in my sacred space, it's enchanting to see the air dance over the altar. The mist reminds me I'm in Avalon protected from psychic attacks and energetic pollution. So having a diffuser as part of your spiritual practice keeps you empowered and connected to the light. Yes, mine comes lit with an array of colors.

Light therapy meets aromatherapy. Hot damn!

ALTAR DECORATION IDEAS

Fresh flowers or plants
Soy candles
Incense or essential oils
Silk or cotton scarves
Dried rose petals
Decorative stands
Gemstone bowls
Photos (especially one of you)
Written notes or affirmations
Soft lighting
Trinket boxes
Totem animals
Crystals
Books
Card decks

UPKEEP

Maintenance s always important. If you let items sit for too long then the energy in the space becomes monotonous and obvious. You become used to how it feels. Growing up, I would always rearrange my bedroom because I got tired of how it felt. Again, it's hitting the snooze button on your intentions and prayers when you don't keep the altar fresh. Then you're left wondering why nothing happened. Well, because you gave up on taking care of the energy. You let the fire fizzle out. Don't blame anyone if your wand backfires on you.

Passion and excitement fuels a lot of magic in the universe. So, if you keep your space tidy, dust free and energetically sound through music or essential oils then the natural chi of your sacred space will build momentum and your life will begin to blossom in interesting ways. This is the main reason why this challenge is broken into weeks instead of months, because we must keep the energy flowing like a river. Most people grow resistant and uninspired about with their space after one week allowing stuff to pile up and collect dust. Remember, your outer world and how you maintain your space is a reflection of your inner world. We preserve what we care about.

Some ways to keep your altar sparkly clean is to include quartz and black tourmaline crystals. These amplify and protect your intent. I love to have Himalayan sea salt around to keep the air positive. But also using essential oils are a great way to diffuse and reinforce your energy for the highest good. One of the things I could change about my color altar experience is using essential oils. Frankincense, cedarwood and clary sage oils energetically shifted my spirituality. Deepened my color prowess and I now have my diffuser as part of my meditation space next to my angel statue so that I can magnify my prayers and intentions using some awesome plant magic in my practice.

My favorite oil in making sure my space feels alive and unblocks my creative resistance is tangerine. Citrus says come out of the closet and be happy. Always make sure the oil energy resonates. And don't be ingesting oils you don't have a clue about. That's something to mention because I don't want to find out you taking shots in front your altar because you saw it online somewhere!

Having more than one person involved grows the energy so if you're building a family or marriage rainbow altar to heal your past, present and future, I mention specific colors, oils and crystals to upkeep and activate your zodiac sign's personality on my blog at (thecolormage.com/zodiac) or flip to the back of the book to learn a little more about color and astrology. Feel free to combine colors if you're trying to balance more than one person's energy in a home based on their astrological sign. My family's mostly water and fire signs, so doesn't that explain all the drama.

If you feel like your space is too cluttered than try the minimalist approach: negative space is free space. White sage is a great auric cleanser but be sure to only use that if you intend on opening a window and letting all the energy out. It's like a reset button that takes out all the negative and positive energy. You will after smudging (cleansing) your space have to add a new vibration to the room. I like to use essential oils and music to fill up the space back up with high vibrational energy.

After I white sage'd my apartment when I moved in, I danced and put on a combination of copiaba and lemon essential oil with the intent to expand the brightness of the room. I love it because as I began dancing with the essential oils diffusing in the air, the sunlight poured right through my window. I felt the walls smile back at me as I danced in the halo of my own happiness.

ALTERATION

Now before you go ahead with your mighty magical self, we need to talk about the flow of energy. Every week you will have to honor and take your time with the objects you decide to pull together in the space. Yes, it's a little more in-depth than just adding all the colors together in one spot and expecting your life to transform overnight. The objects you place together reveal a story reprogramming your relationship to these sacred or cursed artifacts of your history.

All of the tools I use in my space (including books, clothes and jewelry) now have a symbiotic relationship. I go to flip through a book or wear a piece of jewelry used as part of an altar and now feel these are a part of my journey carrying a different kind of magic. It's as though I'm making and destroying *horcruxes* in *Harry Potter*.

These objects contained soul fragments that needed to be destroyed in order to kill he-who-shall-not-be-named. Now, we aren't killing anyone nor are we conjuring a deal with the Devil so you're granted immortality. I feel this experience reconnects you to why you have these household items and trinkets in the first place. Take the wooden roses I got with my ex for example. Those pieces of my altar represented a past life for my soul. That romance energy was still active and living within the spirit of my memories of those two roses. What this altar did for me was give me a chance to destroy the soul fragments keeping that pain point and fear alive inside of me.

I reassigned a new story for myself and threw away the roses because they no longer served my expired fantasies. Your own items will also go through a similar process. The more you wear a piece of jewelry, use an oil or refer to a book that changed your life, you ultimately feed it your life-force by placing soul fragments inside it by making it a part of your life.

This is another reason why my color oracle deck is too overwhelming for some, because every single person is essentially using it and embedding a piece of their own soul inside. What can say, it's been created to keep the real witches and wizards connected in a colorful way. This is another reason why it's important to only choose spiritual tools, essential oils and companies with extreme care. Your energy feeds what you choose to buy and use every single day. Don't be negligent with your life-source. It's the most valuable piece of you.

After bringing all your chosen items together, you want to begin invoking the space with prayer. Now there's no right or wrong way to accomplish this. Ask the Universe or whatever facet of the Divine you're feeling for the day to help you grow and learn from this altar experience. There are books and posts online that talk in detail about calling the corners, opening a full moon circle or chanting 108 times, the how you officially baptize your space is less important for the purpose of this book. You can wiggle your nose three times or cut open four pomegranates naked, I don't care as long as you're gathering the courage to practice your magic using color.

The altars are color coded per chakra making it super easy for you to play the matching game. You can also find a shit-ton of chakra affirmations online (it's a little hard to miss in the new age community) or make your own to summon your power. Again, this is why we have our community and you're more than welcome to chime in and ask what affirmations we're using to stay fierce.

As you transition between colors, you want to reflect and journal about your findings as you live life while these altars are set-up in your space. Notice the subtle shits and miracles that happen as a result of your focus and participation. Let the altars you create to build off of one other is another to understand your journey. Pay attention to memories and current situations that remind you of the objects that get triggered because of your altar. As you move from one from altar to the next take a gift with you whether it's a mantra, memory or feeling.

Color is holistic and not separate because it comes from one source, remember? So use this wisdom to guide you to dig deeper about your own thoughts, chakra levels and personal connection to color.

You're honoring objects and color in your space so that you amplify your energy. Strengthen your aura. Understand the personality of your room better. Feel the magic behind your intentions manifest realities you never even believed you'd experience this lifetime. These elements are the basic ingredients to building the perfect altar because at the end of the day, it's more than decorations and having the biggest most expensive crystal collection. It's about containing your power and using that power for good not evil.

And this revolutionary is why we color.

The Rainbow Revolution Workbook

30 Journal Prompts to Color Beyond Fear

Art freedom and creativity will change society faster than politics

Victor Pinchuk

GRAB A QUILL AND GO

Sit with your altar each week and answer these questions honestly. If you're stuck, be brave and seek wisdom inside the book club. Bonus house points for drawing or creating art with your answers. I left the pages nice and open so you'll have free space to doodle and catch evidence of your magic during this spiritual journey.

Unfortunately, you may have noticed that you didn't get sucked into a multidimensional vortex of light time traveling to a *chamber of secrets* or this book doesn't magically write back to you in creepy inky script either.

Bloody hell!

But definitely have fun and pour your heart and soul onto the paper so that it catches your inner most feelings and thoughts about your experiences with each color altar.

I'd love to see your art journal pages from this workbook so please share your masterpieces inside our book club. Or feel free to tag me on social media, I'm buzzing with excitement already to see your magic unfold.

Swish and flick, let's begin!

FEEL FREE TO PULL OUT YOUR FAVORITE ORACLE AND TAROT CARDS FOR THIS SECTION TO CATCH WISDOM FROM YOUR HIGHER POWER AND SPIRIT GUIDES

THIS WORLD IS BUT A CANVAS TO OUR IMAGINATION

HENRY DAVID THOREAU

WEEK ONE - RED

Red this week makes me feel...

My first memory of this color was when...

If my love life could be anything red, it would be this...because...

The last red thing I ate was....

WEEK TWO - ORANGE

Orange this week makes me feel...

The last time I saw orange, I was afraid of...

Honestly, sex makes me feel like.... but I want sex to feel like this...

My favorite orange colored animal is...

WEEK THREE – YELLOW

Yellow this week makes me feel...

Right now, my body feels and looks like...

If money wasn't an obstacle, I would do this instead of...

This week, I spent time doing...

WEEK FOUR – GREEN AND PINK

Green this week makes me feel...

Pink this week makes me feel...

Love showed up all week, here's how...

Here's what I read, learned or did to expand my personal development...

WEEK FIVE-BLUE

Blue this week makes me feel...

This person is a leader to me because...

Being on social media or hanging out with other people this week made me feel...

If I could help out any charity it would be...because I love this about their mission...

WEEK SIX - PURPLE

Purple this week makes me feel...

My intuition looks and acts like...

My ego looks and acts like...

This week, I was so addicted to...

WEEK SEVEN – WHITE AND METALLIC

White this week makes me feel...

The last time I felt like a diamond was...

I go to church because... or I don't go to church
because...

I know you're no longer with me, but this is what
I miss most about you...

REWIND YOUR JOURNEY
This challenge changed my life because...

My favorite week of this challenge was...because
I got to experience...

The Journey is Over Now What

Keep reading to explore more ways to color and celebrate
your personal magic.

ONLY THOSE WHO
HAVE LEARNED THE
POWER OF SINCERE
AND SELFLESS
CONTRIBUTION
EXPERIENCE LIFES
DEEPEST JOY: TRUE
FULFILLMENT

TONY ROBBINS

RESOURCES AND ALLIES

Here's a legendary list of sources that help me feel the light of my own rainbow.

THE CRYSTAL CAVE

CrystalVaults.com   ContemporaryTara.com

TheWitchyMommy.com   Meta-Essence.com

BOTTLES AND POTIONS

Amazon is a great place to buy books NOT a safe space for real essential oils. Connect with your friend who gave you this book to start your oil adventure. Want an oil hero? Go to thecolormage.com/oils

BOOKSHELF

Radical Self Love – Gala Darling

Easy Breezy Prosperity – Emmanuel Dagher

Stealing Fire – Steven Kotler & Jamie Wheal

The War of Art – Steven Pressfield

White Hot Truth – Danielle LaPorte

What's Your Spirit Animal? - Kelly Eckert

Be The Guru – George Lizos

TO ME WHEN I THINK OF NEW AGE I THINK OF CRYSTALS AND RAINBOWS AND PLATITUDES

MARIANNE WILLIAMSON

NOTES

LGBT statistics you should know about...

[1] http://www.thetrevorproject.org/pages/facts-about-suicide

[2] https://truecolorsfund.org/our-issue/

F.A.Q.

No black? I find black to be invisible and egocentric. I wrote a blog post on the darkest black in the world. Refer to *Appendix A* or vist my blog thecolormage.com

Should I listen to music while building my altars? Totally rock yourself out, here's a playlist I love. Refer to *Appendix B* or go to my YouTube playlist http://bit.ly/ColorMusic

Are only LGBT people allowed to join the revolution? Although I'm gay myself, I welcome all walks of life to experience the power of color. Everyone is welcome.

Omg, I love you, can you please come speak at my event? Why not? Email me hello@thecolormage.com, I love the stage and house parties!

How can I learn to read color? Becoming a certified color reader is easy and a great way to serve more intuition in the world, visit my blog thecolormage.com

COLOR IS FOR ME THE PUREST FORM OF EXPRESSION THE PUREST ABSTRACT REALITY

JIM HODGES

THE DARKEST COLOR IN THE WORLD AND WHAT YOU CAN'T REALLY SEE

Color fascinates me because it's how we perceive the symbiotic relationship of light and darkness.

Our eyes and brain receive messages about the world because of the intimacy created through light and darkness. Ripening fruit and red hot stoves are just a couple of ways we use color to send us a message.

This natural energetic language incredibly texturizes the nooks and crannies of our existence. Making sure we are safe, protected and in balance with planet Earth.

Vantablack is a man-made material producing a color so dark that humans need crinkled foil to see it. Also it's the most expensive color to exist as sources are refusing to disclose price points.

If this material were used to create clothing, we would be black phantoms roaming the world.

So what does this new ultra-black mean metaphysically?

First, you have to decide which side of the spectrum you're on...Do you believe black is a self-absorbed asshole hogging all the light for it's own gain much like a tyrannic politician with a huge ego that trumps your existence as a human being or do you believe black is the absence of any light and color and completely void of existence altogether generally being depicted as a victimized rebel pushing away anything conformist because that's the hipster thing to do?

There's no right or wrong answer.

Both seem to happen equally too for the light side. We're trying to understand two extremes and both have all or nothing attitudes. All for good. All for evil. It's how humanity's been able to wrap it's head and heart around life. In color, it's this balance that keeps morality hanging by the thread of perception. It's your perspective that matters. Your soul's unique awareness that moves through light and dark extremes creates reality. And I help souls navigate aggressively and gracefully when the environments of their adventures shape shift as expected or unexpectedly through the power of color.

Black has always been a misfit in the color world because we naturally associate this dark color to black magic, fear, mystery, uncertainty and death. It's one of the color results in my color quiz, because I feel this particular color deepens our understanding of everything we could possibly fathom appropriately dubbed as the black philosopher which among those that took the quiz over a thousand of you (33% to be exact) are these classic cool observationalists that beat their own drum from the depths of space.

Vantablack broken down as a word means conceited (vanta from Esperanto) and black which is the total absorption of light or complete disregard for it.

Devouring most light this special (undisclosed) military technology black consumes/rejects light with full awareness and intention to the point of vanity, narcissism and egotism.

Of course this is simply coming from the etymology, but the intentions behind creating such a material and color could actually be a subconscious attempt to connect with our deepest darkest regions of awareness.

Good thing though this material absorbs all but 0.035 per cent of visual light.Which tells me that hope still exists like Pandora's box.

Vantablack is more than a breakthrough in nanotechnology, it's a crucial metaphor for our evolution and if we don't mind the natural balance we may lose our innocence and purity completely because true ignorance is only bliss for so long.

ARTISTS CAN COLOR THE
SKY RED BECAUSE THEY
KNOW IT'S BLUE THOSE OF
US WHO AREN'T ARTISTS
MUST COLOR THINGS THE
WAY THEY REALLY ARE OR
PEOPLE MIGHT THINK
WE'RE STUPID

JULES FEIFFER

Appendix B

RAINBOW REVOLUTION

MUSIC PLAYLIST

Idina Menzel – Brave

Jai Jagdeesh – Light of Love

Feist – Intuition

Cowboy Mouth – I Believe

Yuna – Rescue

Eli Lieb – Lightning in a Bottle

Britt Nicole – Gold

Sara Bareilles – Brave

Alessia Cara – How Far I'll Go

Hilary Duff – Chasing the Sun

Joey Graceffa – Don't Wait

Mary Lambert – She Keeps Me Warm

Echosmith – Bright

Katy Perry – Firework

Florence + The Machine – Cosmic Love

Johnnyswim - Diamonds

An unfulfilled vocation drains the color from a man's entire existence

Honore de Balzac

ABOUT THE COLOR MAGE

The wizard behind *TheColorMage.com* and the world's most powerful color therapy deck, *The Color Mage Oracle* is LGBT thought-leader, Bernard Charles. He's a featured color expert in *Soul and Spirit Magazine*, *Medium.com's* LGBT contributor and actively volunteers his time at Pittsburgh's Gay and Lesbian Community Center. When he's not filming epic videos for his Facebook and YouTube following, you'll find him casting spells in massively multiplayer online role-playing games. Bernard is a renowned luminary that carries a fresh unconventional attitude when speaking about diversity, spirituality and color psychology on stage. Add more color to your life by visiting *thecolormage.com*

"I see ordinary people using color everyday to set themselves free and evolve world consciousness." - Bernard Charles

THERE IS NOT ONE
BLADE OF GRASS
THERE IS NO COLOR
IN THIS WORLD
THAT IS NOT
INTENDED TO MAKE
US REJOICE

JOHN CALVIN

HERE'S WHAT OTHERS ARE SAYING ABOUT MY MAGIC

A collection of praise and kind words found on my Facebook page or at thecolormage.com/thankyou

"Bernard is spiritual authenticity at its best, he infuses such exuberance & light into each conversation."

"If you're reading this then the universe has brought you here for a reason. Bernard is the real deal. His color readings are unlike anything I've experienced."

"A true intuitive who does not beat around the bush. He will get to the core of your problem and tell you about it...As an empath and oracle reader myself I can tell you The Color Mage is the real deal!"

"Bernard has such a vivacious and loving personality that he pulls you in immediately... No fake talk, no gimmicks, no bland moments or mundane words being repeated over and over to me. He delivers the truth, the real deal, and lays it out for you in his own quirky beautiful way that I personally can't get enough of. I've had many readings in my 38 years and he certainly has surpassed them all."

"Bernard burst into my life when I was looking to bridge my holistic health knowledge with my spiritual pursuits."

"The results have been profound. In the last month, I left a job that was no longer serving my highest good. It left me tapped of energy and filled with feelings of not enough. I am now moving forward with my own business. I feel freer and more alive."

WORDS ARE CHAMELEONS WHICH REFLECT THE COLOR OF THEIR ENVIRONMENT

LEARNED HAND

THE COLOR MAGE
ORACLE

108 COLOR CARDS TO EMPOWER
YOUR INTUITION AND LIFE

Double dip your intuition. Use *The Color Mage Oracle* as a secondary layer of cards while you read tarot or other divinational tools. There's no guidebook to substitute your actual intuition, but you do receive a 60-minute video training on how to get the most out of your color deck. You can drool over how my color deck is changing lives from around the world on social media #colormageoracle or #colorcards.

GET YOUR OWN DECK:

thecolormage.com

YOUR ZODIAC COLOR

DISCOVER YOUR ZODIAC SIGN'S POWER COLOR

Astrological zodiac signs meet their spiritual color meanings. Find out what color, crystals and essential oils best support you and your partner's horoscope sign. And to guide you deeper along your spiritual path, join the zodiac club. It's my monthly coaching program where I send you personalized video horoscopes and invite you to join exclusive training calls, rituals and access to secret color magic.

LEARN MORE:

thecolormage.com/zodiac

WITH A GRATEFUL HEART

Please allow me to officially acknowledge the alchemy in making this book a reality:

From readers to Facebook friends who message me all the time, you remind me life is worth living. Your comments, testimonials and use of color inspire me.

My mom for making all the right choices. You battled for custody, let me wear a witch costume in third grade, and don't look at me as gay, but see me as happy.

Angela for spending a whole day editing and proofing this book. Yes, I enjoy putting color on a "pedal stool".

Lastly, to the gay soul inside. You single-handedly slay darkness with your light. Guide thousands of souls to honor truth, listen to intuition and love purely. You're the spark behind this revolution. And the real reason I'll never stop believing in the power of love, light and color.

GO AHEAD AND LEAVE ME AN OWL

If you enjoyed this book, found it useful or utterly enchanting then I'd really appreciate it if you would post a short review on Amazon and Goodreads. Actually, if you uploaded a video on YouTube, I'd go nuts over watching it, so feel free to review it anywhere you feel like adding your bad ass light baby! I do read (and watch) all the reviews personally so that I can continually write what people are wanting.

Made in the
USA
Middletown, DE

74868551R00104